STARSEED **- THE AWAKENING**

Yesenia DeCapua

ACKNOWLEDGMENTS

This book was written based on some actual facts of my real life. I felt deeply guided by my star family to share my story with the world in hopes that it will inspire and reach the hearts of so many people especially, the hearts of my brothers and sisters of light that were lost during this process and, still yet have to remember who they truly are and their soul mission.

This book was also written to honor and remember all the peaceful warriors that perished during wars and continue to fight in search of their own divine peace and freedom. To also honor the lost souls that continue to fight the wars within themselves in search of their own unique identity.

Remember, my brothers and sisters, to always look within yourselves for your own divine answers and true divine calling. Listen to your heart. Together, in unity consciousness, we can change the world for we are the creators of our own reality. As Mahatma Gandhi once said *"You must be the change that you wish to see in the world."*

With divine love,

Yesenia.D.

PART 1: THE BEGINNING

ONE

*T*he universe, an immense place filled with vast number of galaxies and star systems we call home, so full of light and highly vibratory energies. Billions of years have passed since the creation of our universe and with that, so many star systems were filled with different life forms some to which grew to become highly evolved beings of light and, others with uniquely complex bodies but with lower vibratory energies. Yet, still in the process of discovering their true inner potentials as beings of light and love.

My name is Araceda, commander of the intergalactic starship of light from the star system your people now call Sirius B. We are highly evolved spiritual beings of light from the 10th dimension. We do not possess denser bodies like many of you do, nor do we require to feed in order to survive. We communicate via telepathic light language. In fact, our bodies are very tall made of pure crystalline blue-like energy of the universe with violet rays that radiates from our crown and foreheads. Our main source of nourishment is the cosmic light from God, creator of all things. Our mission is to help and guide other star systems and their living beings such as your world, to increase their vibratory energy potential, and to advance into a higher dimension of love, unity consciousness, and peace. As your world, or planet begins its evolutionary process, so does also your uniquely complex bodies and spirit begin to change.

We, and many other beings of light from different star systems have been watching your world for millions of years. Watching every single organism go through the complex evolutionary process to become the beings you are now or as you call yourselves "Humans." We prefer to call you all our brothers and sisters, for we all share the same ancestry from our creator whom you also call God. We are all one within the universe. Together with many brothers and sisters from different intergalactic systems, each representing their own unique world, have gathered to create the Galactic Federation of Light. Our sole purpose is to maintain unity of peace and restore balance of all worlds regardless of their spiritual state of consciousness and dimensional evolution. Together with the angelic beings of light such as my brother of light and friend the archangel Michael, have fought against many worlds and beings whose main purpose was to destroy and poison newly develop worlds such as yours, "Earth." For thousands of years we have been very successful protecting your world and many others but, our work is not over yet.

In ancient times, many of us were assigned to visit your world and interact with your people when you were all beginning to take small steps in your intellectual growth. We taught your ancestors many things to get them started such as a little introduction to our technology and where we came from. We taught them where they could find us in the stars and how we were all the same in unity consciousness. You were all so divinely pure souls like babies, innocent and curious, wanting to learn everything about us and never afraid of our presence.

As time passed, we began to slowly withdraw from your presence so that we didn't interfere with your evolutionary process and decision making. Still, we continued to watch you from a distance and we became invisible and undetectable by all of you. With the pass of centuries, you all made great progress in your intellectual and spiritual growth but unfortunately as you expanded your mind, so did also your hunger for power, greed and control of everything that surrounded you. You became destructive against each other, and against all other living beings in your planet for material forms. You forgot your true divinely essence within and became very disconnected from each one of you. We were so deeply saddened by your actions, but still we held a deep hope in all of you. For that reason, many of us were assigned to be your spiritual guides, to help you in some way find your balance within when you most needed it but, in such subtle way so that we did not interfere with your decisions, and you didn't see us.

Our plan of serving you as spiritual guides was working in some way but, still didn't restore the balance within each of you. Your power hunger and self destructive behavior continued to grow in such ways that you began to take control over your own brothers and sisters filling them with fear and erasing every little knowledge left of our existence and of our teachings. With that thirst for control and power, you created a government to brain wash your people and promise things that were not true thus, creating a world imprisoned in your own ego, fear, and lack of true self freedom within. In addition, we felt that there was more to be done soon because your world is to undergo through a major energy shift that could lead to total catastrophe if each one of you did not match that new energy shift of evolution. We might not be able to save all of you, but at least enough of you to get your world restarted. Love and spiritual growth have always been the key for shifting into a higher dimension. Your 3rd dimensional world is soon going to transition into the 5th dimension. Your ancient civilizations like the Mayans, have written about this major transformation which many of your current modern civilizations have mistakenly translated as the end of your world. We'd like to refer to it as the beginning of a new era.

We, the Galactic Federation of Light had decided to do something never done before at the risk of losing many of our brothers and sisters of light, and their divine immortality. We assigned many of our members to descend to your planet Earth as humans, but in order to have a denser body form like all of you, we must be incarnated within you to be able to be born as human beings. Here is where our mission and quest as Star-seeded beings began.

For thousands of years, hundreds of us went on to be born as human beings with the purpose of learning more about you, and get used to our newly denser body forms before the "Big Shift" was to take place. The process was not easy due to many of our brothers and sisters were lost in the transition, and got trapped into karmic cycles, thus reincarnating into many different lives until they were purified, or cleansed from lower vibrations before they could return back to their true home. They lost memory of who they truly were, and their soul mission. Some were so confused, and couldn't tolerate their denser life form, and terminated themselves. Others were hunted to death for possessing abilities unknown to humanity to which you judged them as devil worshipers, or witches. Still, we continued to have hope in all of you, and sent more down to incarnate.

Hundreds of years later, we sent a new wave of Starseeds during the 1950's, 1960's and, 1970's. Many of them lost their true essence and continued to believe that their human body and mind was the only way of existence. They were filled with so much fear and confusion. During the 1980's, another group of Starseeds volunteered to help those lost in the process, and assist them in remembering their true essence of divinity. The new wave of Starseeds from the 80's to your present time, became the most important one of all. They held the key for raising the energy frequencies of planet Earth, and of all its living beings so that it can transition into the 5th dimension. Within them, they brought a new encoded knowledge of coexisting in love, and unity consciousness that was to be re-activated by our brothers and sisters of light when the "Big Shift" was soon to approach. Each of them were assigned with one or several spiritual guides that were with them from the moment they were incarnated, and born as human beings and, with the sole purpose of aiding them with the memories of who they truly are, remembering their mission and re-activating their genetic light code as highly evolved beings of light.

We, the new wave of Starseeds, are the last hope to your current world. Our quest for bringing the new era of evolutionary heart and spiritual transformation has now begun.

Yesenia DeCapua

PART 2 - **THE INCARNATION**

TWO

*H*ave you ever had the sensation that you are being watched by something you cannot see? Well, that has always been my case. I have always been so afraid of the dark like I am expecting to see something unknown to pop out and take me away! (chuckles.) I guess only crazy people like me will think stuff like that.

My mother has always told me that I have been a very unique child maybe borderline weird. Perhaps she was trying to be polite not to hurt my feelings. As a child, I showed many signs of being psychic such as seeing and hearing spirits, angelic beings and also having out of body experiences. I was also able to read, and feel so deeply a person's emotions, and intentions before meeting them which also helped me as a tool in choosing the right people that I wanted to be close to. I remember also that I used to ask her, and my Dad many unusual questions especially about my birth. I used to tell them that they were not my parents, and that I was from somewhere else. Of course, that never went so well because it deeply hurt their feelings. My intention was never to hurt them but, as usual, a child never thinks the stuff they are going to say before they say it. I just had so many things that for some reason I knew, but yet could not understand how I knew them.

My parents, especially my Mom, always tried to reassure me by giving me small talks that a child could comprehend about my birth and how she carried me in her belly for 8 months (Yes! I was a little premature when I was born. I guess I was in a little hurry to get out.) She would tell me stories of how badly my Dad, and her wanted to start a family, but were losing hopes after trying to conceive a child for 4 years. On August 1979, things changed for my parents. A miracle happened, and my brother Joshua was born. She remembers the excitement they both had when he was born. Unfortunately, she said, her child birth was very rough on her to the point the doctors thought they were going to lose her. Even though, she recalls, both of them wanting to have a boy and a girl, they had to make the sacrifice not to opt for that option since it was too risky for my Mom, so they decided to make an appointment with the doctor to have my mother's tubes tided.

Eight months after my brother's birth, and after several months of check ups, my parents returned to the doctor for the actual procedure. The doctor decided to do a very last minute blood work to make sure everything was clear to go. As my mom is being prepped for the procedure, the doctor comes back to tell my parents that they had to cancel the procedure, and instead give her a prescription for vitamins. My parents and the staff were so confused by the doctor's announcement so, as any normal person would wonder, my Mom asked:

"Is there something wrong with me doctor? - Mom asked.

"Everything is great with you! actually more than great! You are carrying a very special life within you! - The doctor reassures.

"What do you mean? I do not understand." - Mom asked with a very confused look on her face.

"Mrs. Zabaleta, you are PREGNANT! Congratulations!" - The doctor cheerfully said.

"But how can that be possible? I just had a child not too long ago! Oh my God! I MUST be dreaming!" - Mom exclaimed.

"Oh! Mrs. Zabaleta, it is more real than you think! You are 3 months pregnant!" - The doctor very thrilled confirmed.

"That is wonderful news doctor! We were not expecting her but we welcome her with all our love." - Dad emotionally said.

"How do you know it's a "she"?" Mom with a surprised look asked my Dad.

"I just know. She is going to be the baby doll you always wanted. You will see." - Dad reassured Mom.

Five months later, on September 1980 in the country of Venezuela, a baby girl was born. Just as my Dad predicted my gender was going to be. They decided to name me Paula after my great grandmother. My parents felt so happy and complete now that they had the pair of babies. They recall me being a sort of an unusual baby, because I constantly slept, and slept and never cried. The only time I would cry, they said, was because they had to wake me up to feed me. My Mom remembers that I didn't even cry when I was born. The doctor had to lightly spank me several times to see if I reacted to that, which I didn't. They noticed I was sucking on three fingers from my left hand and decided to pull my three fingers out of my mouth and, guess what? I finally cried!

When I was 4 years of age, I remember telling my Mom that I was born here for a reason, and that I had a mission to complete but could not remember what it was. My Mom always took the time to listen what I had to say, and encourage me to express myself freely. She always wanted me to see her not only as a mother but also as a friend. She wanted to provide for my brother, and I the affection , love, and support that was never given to her by her parents as a child.

"What makes you feel like that my little tadpole?" - Mom very curious asked.

" I don't know mommy. I just feel I have a mission that I need to complete but can't remember. I feel like the world needs me, and I am here to help people but I don't know how." - I said.

"Those are very intense feelings for a 4 year old baby like you to have my little tadpole! I am very proud of you for sharing that with me. Maybe in time you will learn and remember what that mission is." - Mom said.

"Thank you mommy. I love you!" - I said with a smile on my face.

"I love you too my little tadpole." - Mom said as she leaned to kiss my forehead.

At 5 years of age, I told my parents that I really would like to help people heal themselves so I had made the decision that I was going to be a doctor when I grew up. Both of my parents were shocked to hear this coming from a 5 year old, but supported my decision.

"That is great news my darling! We will support you on anything you would like to do when you grow up, but don't you think you are a little too young to make such a huge decision?. Perhaps, you will change your mind as you get older." - Dad said.

"Honey! Have a little faith in her. Don't fill her mind with doubts." - Mom said.

"Daddy, I know I will not change my mind. I want to help people heal and I think this is the only way I could do it. I have a mission to complete, and I will prove to you that I will not change my mind! You will see!!" - I exclaimed.

"Sorry my sweetie, for saying what I said. I want you to know that I believe in you, and I am very proud of you. I will always be very proud of you. You will always have our support for everything you would want to do in life because we love you." - Dad said as he leaned over to hug me, and comfort me.

"Thank you daddy. I love you too!" - I said as I hugged him back.

Six years have passed since I told my parents about my decision to become a doctor when I grew up, and still held myself so strong with that desire. Now, at 11 years of age, I began to see the world in a more different way. I was so confused, and bothered by modern society's ways of living. I used to get so angry, because I didn't understand why humanity only thinks one way of living is the only way of existing. It bothered me so much that everybody's way of living is to be born, go to school, go to college, get a job, get married, have babies, work until your are old, and fatigued to do anything else and eventually die! It just did not make any sense to me so, of course, I always seek for my parents for answers.

"Mom! Why is that people have to always follow the same routine of life? Why is that we have to go to school to then be working, and get imprisoned in the same cycle everybody follows? Isn't there another way of coexisting? Don't you think there could be something greater for us than just following what people think is real and right? I don't understand after following the same cycles of life, you would think people would have learned to love and respect one another. Why is it that we share the same world but yet we are so distant from each other?" - I asked.

"My little princess, there are things in life that are hard to understand but form part of the reality of life. Unfortunately, we must follow that routine in order to survive, and try to make a difference in this world. We must go to school to learn and be educated, work to have money in order to provide for our families. This is just part of the reality of life. I wish I could have better answers for your concerns. Maybe you could be the one to make the change the world needs! Now, lets start by helping me sweep the floor." - Mom said.

"Yeah..thanks mom! A broom it's all I need to change the world! Maybe I could use it to fly away like a witch and use my magic wand to instantly bring heaven to Earth!" - I said.

"Very funny my little witch! Why don't you start using your magic wand to also help me dust the shelves, and counter tops?" - Mom jokingly said while she laughed.

"sigh....." - I exclaimed with a frustrated look on my face.

PART 3 : *THE WARRIOR WITHIN*

THREE

*F*rom as young as I can remember, my dreams were never about anything beautiful. In fact, they were all about the end of days, war, destruction, terrorism, natural disasters, fire from the sky and the arrival of beings from out of this world. I considered them as visions from the future and not nightmares. I would wake up in the morning scared telling my parents what I had seen. Both of my parents insisted that they were just bad dreams but, I refused to believe so.

One night I had a vision of being in an ancient war fighting to defend a civilization that was being invaded by monsters out of this world. I was holding a sword leading my own army, and next to me was the Archangel Michael with his army of angels ready to battle together against the monsters or demons that were to bring doom to that world. There was so much fire, and so much death. My heart was in so much pain during that vision to see so many of our people fighting to their death for what we strived so much to protect which was peace, and unity. For some unknown reason the Archangel Michael seemed to appear in so many of my dreams/visions, and I didn't understand why. Perhaps, because being raised as a Catholic had to do something with it. I have always had that deep connection with him, and with Jesus. Since then, I began to question my true identity: Who am I? Why do I feel like I don't belong here? Why do I feel like this is not my body, like I am missing something? Why do I feel like I have a family out there in the sky constantly watching me, but yet cannot see them? I felt so lonely, and abandoned.

All these questions not only left me without answers, but also left me questioning my own sanity. I was so confused by all this. I couldn't understand how could I feel like that when I had all the love that a parent could give to their child. One night, when I was 11 years old, I went to bed crying asking God and Jesus to help me find the answer to those questions. I would ask: "Lord! Am I crazy? What is wrong with me? Why do I feel so different from the rest of the people here? Please! Don't leave me wondering without having answers! If you can hear me, please show me a sign!"

Later that night while I was asleep, I was woken up by an intense beautiful bright light coming from the corner of the ceiling of my room. The light then moved from the corner to the center of the room, right at the end of my feet. I was watching in awe, and fear as this light was beginning to take shape from a ball of light to a tall abstract shape, and then slowly began to take a human shape. Beautiful colors of blue, violet, and red began to radiate from the heart center of this being. I just couldn't believe what I was seeing! It was JESUS!

Tears of joy began running down my cheek, and at the same time I didn't want to look at him. I felt like I didn't deserve to look into the eye of such a pure and magnificent being. "My Lord, I am so ashamed to look at you, and I feel that I do not deserve your presence", I said. Jesus with his left hand on his heart, and with his right hand reaching over my chin, gently lifted my head so that I would look at him. He was so beautiful smiling back at me with so much love and compassion. He told me: "My dear one, such a pure soul should never feel ashamed of anything. I love you! Never lose faith and do not let fear overcome who you truly are. Everything will be ok, and I will always be with you in here", pointing to my heart. He then put his hand over my head and left.

His presence, and words were so meaningful to me, and still to this present moment, I carry the memory of that night so vividly engraved into my being. From that day on, I was left almost invincible waking up the warrior within me. Yet, I still felt like there were more unanswered questions that I badly needed to know.

When my brother and I were in elementary, and high school, I always had the feeling that it was my duty to protect him from harm even though I was his younger sister. I saw him as my idol, always wanting to do everything he did. He used to get into a lot fights, I recall. Whenever I saw a crowd of kids in a circle, and I didn't see my brother anywhere, I always got a deep sensation that he was in trouble, and that I needed to rescue him.

"What's going on?" - I asked some kids running towards the circle.

"There is a fight!" - They answered

"Who is fighting?" - I asked.

"We don't know, but we are going there to see!" - They said.

I began to run as fast as I could to get there. I felt as if my heart was beginning to sink into a big hole. As soon as I got there, I heard all the kids screaming: "FIGHT! FIGHT! FIGHT!" and, there he was, my only brother fighting, and being beaten by this kid. I yelled so loudly to the other kids "PLEASE! DO SOMETHING! MAKE THEM STOP!" The kids didn't want to listen as they were so amused by the whole scene. Then, a huge rage overcame my vulnerability, and I jumped into action to protect my brother. I began giving punches, and receiving punches back from this kid. Here is a skinny little girl trying to do the unthinkable:

"PAULA! WHAT ARE YOU DOING? THIS IS MY FIGHT!" - Joshua angrily said with an embarrassed look on his face.

"Hahahaha!!! So look what we have here!! His little sister trying to defend his brother!!! So, Joshua! are you that chicken? hahaha!!!" - The kid fighting Joshua said as he laughed.

"LEAVE HER ALONE YOU JERK! and PAULA! GET OUT OF MY FIGHT NOW!!!!" - Joshua feeling more embarrassed yells as he tries to push me away from the fight.

"NO!!! IF THIS IS YOUR FIGHT SO IT'S MINE TOO, BECAUSE YOU ARE
MY BROTHER!!" - I exclaimed.

He then pushed me out of the fighting ring, and I was left feeling so helpless for him. I began to cry, and then run to find help from the teachers who did not know what was going on. Needless to say, my brother was not very happy with me for what I did. However, that did not stop me from doing the same over, and over again.

We never had such a luck with having friends when we were kids. In fact, we were bullied by the kids from the neighborhood. They used to call us the "Martians" as if they saw a spaceship land into our home. We never understood the reasons for their bullying. Perhaps, because we had such an united family full of love, and support and were raised to respect everything and everybody regardless of their background, or financial status. My Dad always taught us: "Even though you two have the privileges that many other families and their kids can not afford to have, it does not mean that you should treat them any less than you for we are all equal. The greatest wealth does not come from the money you have, but from the humbleness in your heart." I always thought of my dad like a genius, and as wise as Buddha, but he always has a hard time trying to show his emotions. Yet, my Mom, and I always knew how big his heart is.

One night, close to a parking lot that was in front of our home, my brother, me, and some friends were sitting peacefully chatting and having fun when a kid named Joaquin, and his gang of brothers came down to disrupt our peaceful night. He came close to me where I was standing:

"Hey there martian! Aren't you going to invite us to your little party?" - Joaquin asked with a very mischievous look.

"Why should we? Why don't you please go back to where you came from and leave us alone!" - I said with a very commanding tone on my voice.

"Wow!! feeling feisty tonight, huh? That's a nice hair band you have there....now it's MINE!" - Joaquin said with an egotistical sound of voice as he grabs my head and pulls out my hair band from my hair.

"Please stop your stupid little games and give it back to me NOW! OR ELSE...." - I said with a very angry look on my face.

"Or else what? What are you going to do? Are you going to hit me, eh? Bitch!" -Joaquin said with a very daring tone on his voice.

"HEY! YOU BASTARD! WHY DON'T YOU LEAVE MY SISTER ALONE, AND MESS WITH ME INSTEAD! GIVE HER BACK HER HAIR BAND!" - Joshua yelled as he gets up from where he is sitting to confront Joaquin.

"Joshua! Please don't do anything....don't fight!" - I fearfully said as I was trying to keep Joshua away from Joaquin.

They began pushing, and punching each other. I was so frightened when suddenly, a rush of rage and courage filled my entire body, and once again, jumped into action to protect my brother. This time, with a big plan to make the bullying stop once and for all. Most importantly, regain our respect. I started to punch Joaquin back and, I myself, received a punch right straight to the left side of my jaw which in fact, it was meant for my brother, but I took the impact to protect him. Miraculously, I did not feel a thing from that hit and instead, I felt even more powerful to take control over the situation.

"JOSHUA! RUN HOME AND GET MOM NOW!" - I shouted Joshua as I was trying my best to distract Joaquin from hitting Joshua.

"WHY? " - Joshua asked with a very confused look on his face.

"PLEASE TRUST ME! I'M GOING TO BE FINE, BUT YOU MUST RUN AND GET HER NOW! CLOSE THE DOOR BEHIND YOU! QUICK!" - I exclaimed as I was pushing Joaquin out of the way.

"YOU LITTLE CHICKEN BASTARD! GO AND GET YOUR MOMMY, BUT I WILL FINISH YOU FIRST!" - Joaquin angrily shouted.

Joshua ran as fast as he could, and locked the door behind him as Joaquin was approaching the door. Little did Joaquin know what was coming for him.

"YOU LITTLE BASTARD! OPEN THE DAMN DOOR! THIS IS NOT OVER YET. I WILL BEAT THE CRAP OUT OF YOU WHEN I SEE YOU!" - Joaquin yelled as he began to hit and kick the glass door.

"HEY JERK! You are right! This fight is not over yet. Now, it is between you and I. What do you say? or are you too afraid that a girl could beat the crap out of you? Why don't we start by you giving me back my hair band...." - I said with a very confident and fearless look on my face.

"I WILL GIVE YOU BACK YOUR PIECE OF CRAP AFTER I SHRED IT INTO PIECES!!!" - Joaquin yelled as he tried to rip apart the hair band.

"Wrong answer!" - I proclaimed as I charged towards him.

So I locked my fist in position and gave him a strike under his jaw so strong that he seemed disoriented for a couple of seconds. Then, I grabbed him from his hair and scratched his face to eventually give him my final strike, a kick right in between his legs. Meanwhile, all his brothers, our friends and neighbors watched and witnessed in amazement what I had done to him. A girl, by herself, defeating the bully of the group. As expected, I regain the respect for both my brother and I, and guess what? They never messed with us ever again. Using violence to earn respect have never been my first choice, and never will, but this time he deserved it and, I must confess, what a satisfaction and joy that night gave me!

A few years have passed since that eventful night where I regained our respect from the bullies. It is now 1996, and my brother Joshua will soon graduate from high school, and depart to the United States to begin college. He has always been obsessed in studying abroad and especially to the U.S. He taught himself to speak English fluently when he was only 12 years of age. I remember how he used to drive us all crazy playing disks and repeating like a parrot hour after hour his English lessons. I have always had a deep admiration for the passion, and determination that he puts to the things he loves, and wants to do. Even though, letting him go at the young age of 17 to a far away country was not an easy decision for my parents to take, because we were all going to be apart from each other but, they were willing to support his wishes in the name of love and began to look for U.S college representatives for him. Successfully, he was able to enter to a university of his like, and left to the state of Ohio to a very small town named Findlay.

We felt that our family was getting smaller and smaller. We missed Joshua so dearly. Even though he would call us every weekend, it was not the same as having him in person. One year after his departure, in 1997, I began to question myself again: Why is it that after all this time I still don't feel like I belong here in this country, this world? Why do I feel so strange in my own skin almost as if I didn't use to have a solid body before? Is there more that I need to learn and discover about myself that yet I don't fully know? Why do I feel like my home country is not the place to provide me with those answers?

My brother convinced me to go the U.S to study at the same University he was attending and, on July 1997 at the age of 16, I left my country to begin my new journey. I didn't even attend my high school graduation, but the only thing that hurt me the most was leaving my parents by themselves behind knowing how much they would suffer, especially my mom. She, and I always had this deep inner spiritual bond. We were always so close like best friends. Their love for us has always been so strong that they sacrificed their feelings for our happiness. They always wanted the best for us, and were willing to provide for us no matter the cost to make that happen.

"My little princess, are you sure that going there is what you really want to do? Is there anything else I could do to convince you to stay?" - Mom tearfully said.

"Mommy, I know how hard this must be for you and Dad. Trust me, I feel the same way too and believe me, I'm afraid too! There is this thing burning within me that I have yet to discover, and I know I have so much potential within me waiting to get out. I feel so deeply guided that this is the only way for me to find out the answers that I'm seeking. I have always felt that I don't belong here, and I'm not like the rest of people. I need to find out if there are more like me somewhere else."- I said with a very sad look on my face.

"I understand my princess. I so hope that you are right, and find what you are looking for. I respect, and admire your decision. Remember, we will always be by your side to support you no matter what happens."- Mom said.

"Thank you mom. It means the world to me to know that I have your support." - I said as I tried to hug my mom.

We said our goodbyes at the airport. It was such an emotional moment for all of us. I could feel so deeply my mom's heart breaking into pieces, but I knew deep within me everything was going to be ok, and that I was making the right decision.

Everything was working really good for me in the U.S., and I became very fluent in the English language in just 1 month. I had tons of friends, and everybody made me feel like a goddess! My grades were excellent. I found quite interesting that I seemed to understand, and study better in a totally different language than mine. In fact, even math and physics made more sense! I was awarded Dean's list student during my first two semesters and continued to excel throughout my academic year. Due to my excellent grades, my father decided to keep me studying in the U.S so that I could pursue my degree in medicine. After one and half year of being in college, and studying so hard, my emotions of missing home, confusion of who I really was, and what is expected of me soon took a toll on me, and sent me deep down into the abyss. I couldn't concentrate in school, didn't want to eat, and couldn't sleep. Everyday I would come to my room, and cry in agony for no reason. Many times my brother would find me on the floor on a fetal position screaming in pain. He had to slap me on the face several times to make me comeback to reality, and then he would pick me up and hug me feeling helpless for me. I was now fallen into a major depression so severe that I contemplated committing suicide.

Out of desperation, I sought help with the school counselor. I knew that committing suicide was not the answer, and it was just a selfish decision from my part to get rid of my pain when in fact, it could potentially create a domino effect destroying, and dragging with me all the people that I cared, and loved the most. Now I was fighting another bully and, this time, that bully was inside of me.

My first session with the school counselor was not as easy as I was expecting. I thought she would make me feel like I could trust her or make me feel more comfortable, and instead I felt like there was a huge distance between us. I felt as she was guarding herself from not showing any feelings or emotions towards me. It was such an awkward moment especially when she wanted me to tell her about my life, and what is bothering me.

I have never been very good at telling the insides and outs of my mind, and soul to a complete stranger especially someone who seemed so cold, and distant. I began to get very flustered, and like I was being cornered. Suddenly, all these emotions exploded like lava from a volcano, and I began to cry so bad that I couldn't even talk. I told her all these things hidden within me, all the sorrow and pressure that I was experiencing. Meanwhile, she was there sitting and listening to everything I was saying and, at the same time, she was giving me a bewildered look as if I was a nutcase. She told me that she was going to review our conversation with a physician to see if they can prescribe me a medication for depression and anxiety and go from there.

After a couple of weeks of taking the medications, things did not change, but they got worse. I called the counselor to arrange another session urgently, because I did not know how long I could hold on to that sensation of sorrow.

"Paula, I really do not know what else to do for you. I am not a Doctor, and what I can only offer you is guidance and listen to what you have to say. I can only tell you that you have a very severe case of depression, and very soon I might have to refer you to a psychiatrist, and admit you to a special clinic for cranial electrotherapy treatments. If you like, I can call the specialist now and get you started with the admission papers." – The counselor said.

I was left speechless, hopeless and more so betrayed. I had a rush of mixed emotions within me with my rational frightened mind trying to get out, and make the decision for me to get admitted. Suddenly, an inner voice told me: "Do NOT sign any papers! You CAN fight this on your own! You are not alone....you have never been. We are here to help you, and you will succeed for there is a warrior built within you! Never lose faith, dear one!"

"I think I made a mistake coming here. I thought you could be someone I could trust, and could help me. I will not sign any papers, and I'll try to deal with this on my own." – I said

"I understand. Call me if you need anything else, and set up another appointment to check on your progress." – The counselor said with a very surprise look on her face.

I began my process of healing with prayers begging God, and Jesus to illuminate my path and make me stronger during the process. I started a routine of exercises everyday running the track in school, going to the library to study, or read so that I wouldn't feel alone. I felt like Rocky Balboa training for the biggest fight ever. Within a few days, I began to feel better, and people out of nowhere would come and join me. It felt as if God was sending me angels to keep me company and keep me strong. One week later, I was fully recovered and depression free! I was freed and won another battle once again! I then went to see the school counselor to show her my remarkable improvement:

"So, how are you feeling Paula? Have you decided if you want to see the psychiatrist that I mentioned to you, and be admitted?" - She said.

"As a matter of fact, I am doing great..... more than great, and I do not need a psychiatrist. I am cured and my depression is gone!" - I said.

"But how is that possible? About one week ago you had a severe case of depression that needed special attention....nobody that has had your level of depression has recovered that quick with no treatment?" - She said.

"Well, what can I say, I have beaten the odds."- I said.

"How did you do it? Did someone else help you in your recovery? Did you see a specialist?" - She asked.

"Well, my will for getting better was stronger than my own problem, and I couldn't also have done it without the divine intervention of God. What can I say, I have always been protected." - I said as I was getting up to leave.

PART 4 : *THE SOUL SEARCHING QUEST*

FOUR

It is now December 2002, and I have become even stronger and more determine than before. I kept my mind so focus by burying myself with books and studying very hard. I kept myself so busy that I disconnected myself from my soul searching. I blocked myself from my own psychic abilities out of fear that it would bring me back to feeling confused again. Yet, sometimes I would find myself walking outside in the dark, on my way back to my apartment, looking at the sky, and the stars wondering why I keep having this deep sensation that I am being followed from up above in the sky by something that I cannot see, and that was familiar to me. I would then smile as I'm looking at the sky, and shake my head like I was crazy for thinking things like that.

My school year is soon to be over, and I am now scheduled to do my internship for eight months at a Hospital in the city of Toledo, Ohio. My dreams of becoming a doctor were postponed due to my current status as a foreign student. I had to change my major from Pre-medicine to Nuclear Medicine. I knew that if I graduated as a pre-medical student, I wouldn't be able to find a job while waiting to get into medical school which made my chances of getting in very difficult. Now, with Nuclear Medicine, I was still in the medical field, and I was going to fulfill my dream of working at a hospital with patients. Most importantly have a job that could sponsor me to stay in the U.S legally, and earn some experience.

I was very scared to move alone into another city that was not familiar to me, but at the same time very excited for the next chapter in my life. All I kept telling myself that technically I was not alone because I have a boyfriend named Tony whom I was already dating for six years, and my brother who still lived in Findlay which is about 45 minutes from Toledo. Unfortunately, I did not get to see Tony very often because he was working in another state. Our relationship was constantly apart from each other, but we talked on the phone almost everyday.

He is such a smart, and kind hearted person, and I am so thankful for having him in my life. He has made me grow in many positive ways and has helped me in times that I most needed it. However, I was beginning to have doubts if he was ever going to be ready to propose me in marriage, and if I was ever going to be good enough for him.

Two months have passed now since I moved to Toledo, and I was so thrilled each day to be working, and helping real patients. I was so busy everyday with my internship and case studies that I had to do for my school every month. I felt that I had to find something else to do besides work, and study so I began looking for places nearby to work out. Unfortunately, I wasn't able to find a health club close enough to my apartment, and the only one I found, I wasn't too crazy about it. I went home to think about it before making my decision.

One night, I was shuffling through my mail to throw away some advertisement papers that I received, and at the same time I was thinking, and wishing to find a closer place to work out. Suddenly, as I'm holding the mail that I was going to throw away, a small rectangular green flyer falls down to the floor. As soon as I bend down to pick it up, I noticed that it was a flyer for a health club, and to my surprise it was 5 minutes from where I live! It was so weird almost like a sign that I was to go there.

The next day, I went to see the place and get some information. So far the place looked nice, and the girl that was attending me informed me that she was going to have one of their representatives show me around.

"Hey! Daniel! I have a girl interested in the club, and would like a tour. I know you are new here but, would you feel comfortable in showing her around? Maybe she could be your first client." - The girl said.

"I have no problem in showing her around. I feel confident enough about the stuff you guys taught me" - Daniel replied.

"Awesome! If you have any questions let us know. Good luck!" -The girl said.

Meanwhile, I was there still sitting and looking around when I saw this guy coming to get me. I was thinking to myself "hmmm...ooh lala!..cute guy!"

"Hi, my name is Daniel and I am one of the representatives. How are you doing today?

"I am doing great thank you for asking. My name is Paula."

After our introduction, I had this deep sensation that there was a connection there for the way he was looking into my eyes. He began showing me around the club, and trying to get to know me better. He seemed very curious, and interested about me. He noticed my light Spanish accent, and wanted to know even more about me. We were getting along very well, and talked so many things besides the health club. I felt that night could have been the beginning of a nice friendship. As the weeks passed by, I continued to go to the health club to work out, and Daniel kept coming to me to greet me and talk to me. I began to notice that he had a crush on me. I was so flattered by it, but at the same time nervous that it would create problems, and distraction for my school work, and my current relationship.

Daniel was never very shy to show his feelings towards me, and was very clear in letting me know he liked me. I expressed my gratitude for his sincerity, and openness, but I had to be clear to him that I was already in a relationship, and wanted to be friends only. I could notice the disappointment in him, but respected my intentions to be friends. For several months we continued our friendship at the club, and at the same time Daniel couldn't help to hold his feelings for me. Even, all his coworkers already knew about how crazy he was for me. He always had a way to widely open his heart to me like nobody else has done it. Every time he would express his love for me, it would reach so deep into my core, and I began to get so confused about my own feelings. One night after my work out, I was heading out to the parking lot to get into my car to go home when suddenly I heard my name being called:

"Paula! Wait!" - Daniel said as he is running towards me.

"Hey! What's up?" - I said.

"I just didn't get a chance to tell you good night. You look so beautiful tonight...the moonlight makes you even more beautiful. I am sorry that I keep telling you how I feel about you, and I know you made it clear that you only want to be friends, but I cannot help it. You drive me crazy! I can't stop thinking about you. The more I get to know you, the more I feel like I am falling in love for you, and right now I really wish I could kiss you" - Daniel said as he placed his hand over my face to caress me.

I was speechless, my heart was racing, and my legs felt as if they were going to give up on me. I am now looking into his eyes, and feeling like a teenager that was going to get kissed for the first time. I really don't know what happened, but I was caught up in the moment. I found myself into his arms and we began to kiss. It was such a sweet, and emotional moment that I forgot my present reality. I then went home still thinking about that moment when suddenly I received a phone call from Tony. Reality then came crashing down on me, and I was so scared. I was beginning to regret what happened that night. I felt so awful, and angry with myself. I talked to Tony for a little bit trying not to show anything that he might suspect that there was something wrong with me. The next day, I went to talk to Daniel about what happened that night. I wanted to make a stop to it:

"Daniel, what happened yesterday was a mistake, and cannot be repeated again. I appreciate you being so honest with me, but I cannot afford to complicate my life nor distract myself from my school work, because that is my main focus right now. I've been in a relationship for the last 6 years, and I do not think it's fair, or appropriate that I do this behind my boyfriend's back. I could only offer you my friendship, and I hope you can understand."

- I said while inside I was feeling fearful that I could lose Daniel for good.

"I understand how you feel. However, I do not regret what happened yesterday, because it was the best moment in my life. I am sorry that you feel that way, and I respect your current status. I don't know if I can only be friends with you, because I can no longer hide my feelings, but you have my word that it will not happen again." - Daniel said.

"Thank you for understanding. I hope I don't lose you as a friend. Who knows maybe in time things will change for you, and you will find someone else that will sweep you off your feet." - I said.

"I doubt it for there is not many like you with such beauty, grace, intelligence, beautiful heart, kind, funny, and many more. You are one of a kind! All in one package. Your boyfriend is very lucky to have you, and I sure hope that he appreciates what he has....a complete treasure." - Daniel said.

I tried so hard not to lose it, and start crying. I just looked at him and smiled feeling horrible, and wondering if the mistake that I was making was not taking a chance or leap of faith with him. We then went on with our everyday lives, and he stayed true to his word, but once in a while he couldn't help to express his feelings for me. One time we sat down to talk, and he told me that he went on a date with a girl that badly wanted to go out with him. I couldn't help, but to feel a little jealous, and I did my best to hide my feelings.

"So, tell me, how did your date go." - I asked nervously, and scared to hear something that I didn't want to hear.

"It went really well. We went to a gay bar though." - He said

"A gay bar? But what kind of a date is that? That's not romantic at all! Why did you take her there?" - I said.

"Well, it was not my idea it was hers. She wanted to go there, because she has some friends there that are gay" - He replied.

"Hmmm...Interesting. I imagine you got hit on a lot!" - I jokingly said.

"Oh! I really do not want to talk about that!" - He said while he begins to laugh.

"So, are you guys going to see each other again? How did the night end? Did you guys kiss? Was there a connection?" - I asked

"Nothing happened that night. I could tell she wanted to kiss, but I didn't let it happen. To tell you the truth, I don't know if I will go out with her again. Don't get me wrong, but she seems like a nice girl, but she is not you. I couldn't help, but to think of you the whole time. I really cannot get you out of my mind, and my heart. My heart now belongs to you only." - He said.

I gulped back my emotions feeling speechless, and at the same time glad that nothing happened between them. Three years have passed now, we began to get closer, and closer each day, or as I called it our supposed "friendship." I talked to my mom about my new friend so many times that she already knew all about him. She began to question me:

"Are you sure you guys are only friends? It kind of seems to me that you are beginning to develop love for him. Be very careful in what you are doing, because you are playing with fire, and if you don't clear your feelings as to what you want, you could be left without one, or the other." - Mom said.

"NO! Mom! I am not falling for Daniel. I only see him as a friend and I know what I'm doing." - I replied.

"Hmmm....I sure hope you know what you are doing, because as your mother, I know you so well like the palm of my hand, and I deeply feel that there is a storm of emotions building up inside of you.....and that storm has a name, and it is Daniel." - Mom insistently said.

"MOM! You are nuts! - I said jokingly, but at the same time feeling very confused that she could be right.

One night, around two in the morning, I woke up in fear after having a horrible dream, and I was feeling like I was not alone in the apartment. I felt like I was being watched by an entity that I could not see, but yet could feel it very heavily. I could not stop, but to immediately pick up the phone and call Daniel.

"Daniel! I am so sorry to bother you, and wake you up, but I am so frightened! I don't want to be alone....I am so scared! - I desperately said.

"What happened? Are you ok?" - He said very concerned.

"I just had a bad dream, and I am very scared....I don't know what to do!" - I said.

"Ok...I'll be right over....in 10 minutes. Just try to relax and wait for me." - He said.

"Ok...thank you so much" - I said.

He then arrived, and I explained what has happened to me. I confessed to him something that I was always afraid of telling other people out of fear that they would think that I was crazy. I told him that I have psychic abilities, and that I knew that there was a being that has always followed me everywhere I went, and that I always felt his presence. He seemed very surprised, but didn't question my confession. Most importantly, he believed me. We then slowly began to fall asleep on the couch. Now, more than before, I began to believe what my mother was trying to warn me....I was falling in love with Daniel.

It is now August 2003, I have now completed my internship, graduated from school, and living permanently in Toledo. I am now working full time at another hospital, and excited for my accomplishments. I still remained "friends" with Daniel. My long time boyfriend, Tony, of eight years now, was coming to visit me, and with that he brought a surprise. He prepared a picnic style dinner in the living room and then, he popped the question: Would you marry me? I was so shocked with mixed emotions of happiness, and confusion. I couldn't stop thinking about Daniel, and that I was going to break his heart. I looked at Tony, and my answer was "Yes."

I did not know how I was going to break the news to Daniel so I kept it secret for a week, or so when suddenly, Daniel stopped by my hospital department just to say hi, and I accidentally touched my face using my hand with the engagement ring showing. He saw it, and became pale, and with disbelief he asked:

"Is that an engagement ring? Are you engaged?" - He asked sounding really hurt.

"Yes, Daniel. I got engaged, and I was going to tell you, but I did not know how to break the news to you." - I sadly said.

"I don't know what to say....Congratulations! I hope that he makes you happy.....I got to go now I am sorry....." - He then walked out choking up on his own emotions.

I felt so horrible, and so confused if accepting the proposal was the right decision. I couldn't tolerate the fact that Daniel was hurting because of me, and I missed him so dearly. Days had passed, and I didn't have any contact with him until one day we got together, and talked.

"Daniel, I am so sorry for not telling you about my engagement. I did not want to hurt you nor did I want you to find out about it the way you did. I really don't want to lose you....I miss you! I am so confused about this whole situation!" - I said tearfully.

"You don't know how much I would want you to spend the rest of your life with me instead. I have fallen so hard in love with you! I know that deep inside you have feelings for me.....Why don't you take a chance with me? I will love you like no other, and make you the happiest woman ever!" - He said.

"Because I am so afraid that I am going to make a mistake. I am afraid that if I go with you, you might change, and not be the beautiful person that you are now." - I said.

"That will never happen.....I promise you that!" - He affirmatively said.

So there I went. After several weeks of thinking, and rethinking my feelings, I realized my love for Tony had slowly diminished with the passing of time, and distance. My attachment to him was more like the love for a brother. I had so much to appreciate him for he was there helping me in the times that I most needed it for so many years, but I grew so apart because of so many years of being so away from each other. I realized that even though we became engaged, he had no intentions of getting married any time soon for he thought it was not the right time. To me, this only meant more years of waiting. Meanwhile, losing someone that thought of me as big enough of treasure to have.

I then made a decision. I decided to take a leap of faith, and follow my heart. I broke off my engagement with Tony, and went with Daniel. All I can say is that Daniel was the happiest man ever, and couldn't stop promising me that I will not regret my decision, and that he will make me the happiest woman alive. I was so happy, but couldn't help to feel hurt for Tony. After all, Tony and I shared so many memories, and so many experiences together. My rational mind was trying to overcome my heart making me feel confused if I made the right decision. I did go on with my new life, and everyday falling more in love with Daniel. As he promised, he never changed, and instead was getting better and better. He made me feel like a princess each day.

One year later, on September 2006, we got married. We had the most beautiful catholic ceremony ever, and I was filled with so much joy and bliss. My parents came for our wedding, and my Dad got to walk me down the aisle. It was such an emotional moment for all of us. Now, with the passing of time our love became even stronger, and more closer than ever before. As the old saying says "Love is patient", and Daniel is the proof of that for he had to patiently wait three, and a half years to have my love.

Everything seemed to be so perfect for me, I have the love of my life, beautiful, and supportive parents, a wonderful career, a job, I modeled, and then began ballroom dancing competing nationwide. You would think that I had the life that anyone would dream of, but instead, I felt like something else was missing. I felt as if there was still a hole that needed to be filled, but did not know what it was. I let that empty feeling linger for a few years when suddenly things came crumbling down on me once again.

PART 5 : *THE AWAKENING*

FIVE

*I*t is 3:33 am, and I just got woken up by a very strange, and unique dream. It felt so real as if I was really taken, and then broke back into my room making me feel so disoriented. It took me a few seconds to realize that I was really in my room with Daniel next to me. I dreamed that a very tall being, about 7 or 8 feet tall, from out of this world came to get me, and took me inside this spaceship made of a material that I have never seen before. It almost look like a metal that emitted pure energy light, and became invisible when in contact with Earth's atmosphere. It did not make any sound. As I walked inside the ship with this being, I noticed that there were at least seven other tall beings observing my presence, but in a way as if they knew me, and were welcoming me. I followed the tall being to the front of the ship where it seemed like the control center. I saw many strange writings that were glowing in red, and for some reason they looked so familiar to me, but couldn't remember. In the middle of the control center, there was this big energy field made of many different light colors, and it seemed like it was powering the ship. There were also holographic images of our solar system. I couldn't help to notice that I could only see the silhouette of these beings, and couldn't see how they really look like so I asked the being that came to get me:

"Why can't I see how you all really look like? Why am I here, and where are you taking me?" - I calmly asked.

"We believe you are not ready to see how we really look like, but in time you will be able to see us better. This is the best way we could show ourselves to you so that we didn't frighten you. We brought you here, because we want to help answer the questions you always had since your childhood." - The tall being said.

Our conversation was all done via telepathy. I walked close to a window on the ship, and noticed that we were leaving Earth and were traveling so fast through space. I couldn't help to notice the beauty of the different galaxies, and star systems we were passing so full of many colors ranging from pure violet, red, blue, and golden lights. I felt so much love coming from those lights in the universe. The tall being was there standing next to me, and at the same time looking at me as if he was reading my thoughts, and feelings. I didn't feel threatened by him. In fact, I felt so much love coming from him as if we were family.

"Where are we going?" - I asked.

"We are going to show you a very special star system in which a single planet went through a major evolutionary transformation, and all the strongest living beings adapted to the change to become highly evolved beings of love and light. We know how curious, and confused you have been, and we hope that what we are going to show you will help you answer some of your questions." - The tall being said.

He then, at the command of his hand, pulled a hologram showing me two separate star systems, or galaxies on the verge of collision. As the two galaxies came in contact with each other, and their outer layers began to entangle, all the planets broke apart from their orbits making some of them collide with each other. After millions of years, the two galaxies became one forming a new star system where the living beings of one single planet survived, and adapted to the new evolutionary change.

We then descended into that planet, and once we landed, the tall being took me outside the ship so that I could look around. I was amazed to what I was seeing. There was so much beauty, and colors of violet, blue, and pink over the sky. As I am looking at the sky, I noticed that I could see other moons, another big planet so close to the planet we were in, and two suns. The suns were not as strong as ours. The light, and heat were so subtle and loving. I saw other creatures walking around, and they were beautiful. Their skins were blue with violet, and at times it almost looked like they glowed. I was feeling so emotional from all the beauty that I was seeing that tears came down my face. The tall being then put his hand on my shoulder, and telepathically told me that it was time to go.

The dream felt as If I was really gone for hours. I was so perplexed from my experience that I couldn't stop thinking about it. I began to question myself if the experience I had was not a dream, and if it really did happen. The questions I have always had since my childhood about my real identity came to resurface again, but I did my best to suppress my feelings, because of fear that I will lose my sanity, and what people would think about me. I continued to wake up about the same time every night. Sometimes I would wake up around 11:11 pm, 12:12, 3:33 am, 4:44 am, and 5:55 am. Not only I would wake up to see the same numbers, but also I would see them during daytime. Every time I would turn to look at the clock, the same numbers would appear. I began to wonder if they had a special meaning, or if there were messages encoded within those numbers, but I never took the time to investigate, and opted for ignoring them.

A couple years have passed since that unique dream experience I had, and I continued to go on with my daily life routine. One day, on January 2008, I was at work finishing a study on one of my patients, and I noticed my patient needed help getting off from the scanning table. I went to help him so that he could have an arm for support as he pushed himself up. The action of helping our patients get up from the scanning table was very common for us at work due to our scanning tables unfortunately don't have anything for the patient's to hold on to, and help themselves get up. Unfortunately, this day was the one that made all the happiness left in me crumble down on me like an avalanche. As I am helping my patient get up, my patient began to lose balance and thus, making me hold all his body weight. I began to feel as if the last vertebral disk on the left portion of my lower back was oozing fluid and crushing my disk. I began to instantly experience pain, but I was glad to have being able to prevent the patient from falling to the floor.

From then on, my life and happiness went downhill. I was beginning to feel like a bird whose wings have been cut, and could no longer fly. Not only was I fighting the pain, and frustration from my injury, but also the pain of finding out that I was being betrayed by my own work place. I thought that after working hard for so many years that I would find more support, and respect from the institution, and instead they were looking for any way possible to make me look like I was faking it by sending people to spy on me. I began to fill myself with anger, frustration, and sadness. Everyday after work, I would come home crying, because I began to see my work as a big lie full of negativity. I began to discover how money, and power can change the hearts of people by making them disconnected from one another. I was now sinking myself into a deep dark hole. The questions of what my mission here on Earth really is, and who I really am came to resurface again. After two years of feeling lost and abandoned, on the night of November 2010, I was woken up by two tall beings calling my name:

"Paula.....It's time to wake up." - The two tall beings gently said.

"What do you mean? It's not the morning yet!" - I said half asleep.

"Paula...It's almost time, and you need to prepare. We need you." - The two tall beings said.

"Prepare for what?" - I asked.

"In time you will understand, but you must prepare soon" - They said but in a way as if they were smiling.

I was getting ready to ask them one more thing when I noticed that they had disappeared. That night left me as if a light switch was turned on me. It was like a wakeup call to remember who I am, and my soul mission. I was feeling like tons of information was downloaded into my being and everyday I was seeing sparkles or light in front of me, some so big with silver-blue, and violet colors that almost look like a window from another dimension was going to open. I was again regaining my strength, and more determined to find more answers. I knew that nobody else like regular people could help me, and that I had to find people like me. I began searching online for information, and people who had the same, or similar experiences like mine. What I found was the answer to all my questions. Not only I knew that I was a psychic empath, but now I know that I AM a Starseed. A being from another dimension, or star system who incarnated on Earth as a human being in order to fulfill a mission to help humanity on to the next step of evolutionary consciousness, and move them on to the next dimension. I felt as if a heavy bag was lifted off my back. I was so happy to find out I was not alone, and there were other people like me....other Starseeds. Everything now made more sense, and the beings that kept visiting me were my star family trying to help me regain the memories of who I really am, and what my soul mission is. I was not afraid anymore and, now more than ever, I wanted to learn more how to use better my psychic abilities, and meet other Starseeds.

I started to go to psychic workshops where I learned that I have two spirit guides: Archangel Michael, and Krishna. I began preparing myself by meditating everyday in order to increase my vibrations, and regain energy, strength, and asking in prayer for the assistance of my two spirit guides so that I could speed up my growth process. From then on, my life seemed more brighter, and more meaningful. It seemed like every path I took was being cleared for me, and I was feeling stronger each day, more filled with joy, and more connected to the love of God. Mother Nature became my second home, and I was connecting so much more with her during my meditations. I would sit, or lay on the grass, and feel so welcome by her, and so much so that butterflies, dragonflies, and even a rabbit would come to greet me where I was sitting.

From the moment I found out about my real identity, I was comfortable enough to reveal my truth to Daniel. I knew that there could be a slight chance that he might think that I was losing my mind, but I was ready to come out of the closet. At first he didn't know what to say, but more so curious to know more about my identity. I knew that explaining such a thing was not going to be easy for other people to understand especially talking about beings from out of this world incarnating on Earth as human beings. Fortunately, Daniel has always been very supportive during the whole process, and most importantly, he believes in me.

One night I was woken up by extreme tremors in our room. I thought it was an earthquake, but when I turned to look at Daniel he was deeply sleeping as if nothing was happening. Meanwhile, the room kept shaking, and suddenly the entire room was engulfed in a golden bright light that I've never seen before. I then knew that I was being visited again. As I am sitting on the bed admiring this bright light, and at the same time I couldn't help to feel a little bit of fear, I saw these light beings entering the room, and all of them about 5 feet tall. They all look so bright, and shiny, but I could still see their eyes as they were looking at me. Some of them went to grab, and touch my legs, and feet, and I began to panic. As soon as they saw that I panicked, one of them approached me, and stood next to my left arm placing his hand on top of my left shoulder, and telepathically told me not to be afraid, because they were there to help me activate my genetic light code. He then gave me the sweetest loving smile that I have ever seen, and I began to relax letting them do their work.

My process of awakening seemed to be going at ultra fast speed. I was beginning to feel more alive, and more in-tune with my true self, loving every single breath I took, and every ray coming from the sun. I now understood that there was a reason for my back injury, and it was to awaken me to who I really am, and give me the courage, and strength to move on to my divine path, to set myself free from the corporate world. It is all about divine timing, and now is my time to fulfill what I came to do in this world.

PART 6: *THE CONTACT*

SIX

*I*t's been 12 years since the last time I went back to my beloved country Venezuela. Even though my parents had come to visit us here in the U.S every year for Christmas, and New years, it is not the same as going back, and be present to see them in my own home land, and to bring back all those wonderful childhood memories. In some way, deeply within my heart I wanted to go back to show Daniel for the first time where I was born, and lived half of my life, but at the same time I was fearful to return perhaps for fear of confronting a part of my old me that was left behind, and the current political dictatorship that my beloved country was going through. Daniel did all his best to convince me to take him to my home country, and finally succeeded upon several months of constant begging.

On September 2011, we were on our way to Venezuela. I was feeling an immense joy, and fear at the same time. It almost felt as if I had a thousand butterflies in my stomach. My parents couldn't wait the moment we stepped out the plane. They were so excited including Daniel. We had a very interesting flight. We were supposed to arrive to our destination around 9:00 pm, but due to an unexpected conflict inside the plane during midair by two aggressive drunk passengers, our plane was forced to return back to Atlanta. As soon as we landed, the police forced themselves into the plane, and escorted the two passengers out of the plane, and to jail. Not only did we have to forcefully land back to Atlanta, but also all of us had to wait to board another plane which was not available until 11:30 pm. By the time we finally left Atlanta for the second time, we were able to reach safely to our destination at 3:30 am. We were exhausted, but the long flight wait was worth it after seeing my parents waiting for us at the airport with their big smiles. It was such an emotional moment to stand once again on the grounds of my beloved country, and it felt like a dream.

The next day of our arrival, we began our journey in my homeland. My Dad had a two week itinerary to take Daniel on a tour of almost the whole country with each day visiting a different state. We were all so excited to travel together as a family once again, and I was filling myself with so many wonderful memories. I was feeling like a child during those moments. Daniel was amazed by the beauty my country had to offer, and especially the white sand beaches, so much so that the poor guy burned himself like a lobster! He could barely walk, because his feet were so red, and swollen from the sun, but that is what happens when you are warned, and you don't listen. Thankfully, my Mom knows a lot about natural medicine, and treated him with pure aloe vera crystals, and in a matter of 3 to 4 days his feet were almost back to normal.

We continued our journey through the remainder of the country, and this time we were heading to my hometown to visit some family members, and go to the condo where we lived, and I grew up until I was 16 years old. I was so emotional, because there were so many wonderful memories, and beautiful energy in there. In there is where everything about me began, where I knew I had a mission to fulfill, where I saw Jesus, where I discovered my supernatural abilities, where I had bad days, and happy days. The old me was now meeting the new me, and it was time to say our good bye.

It is almost time for us to return back to my second home country the U.S., and I couldn't leave without telling my parents about the discovery, and remembrance of my true divine self at the risk that they might think that I was losing my mind, or involved in a cult. At the beginning, my Mom was so confused by all that, and at the same time did not take it so well especially when I resurfaced the subject that I am not from this world. My Dad was listening attentively to what I had to say without questioning me, but accepting me as I am whether he believed the story, or not. He has never been a big believer of supernatural phenomena, or unworldly things.

"Since you were a child you always questioned your human identity, and that we were not your parents, which that deeply hurts my feelings. I could not understand how you were coming out with those things especially after giving birth to you, and carried you in my belly for 8 months! I was so glad that after a few years you stopped saying those things, and I cannot believe that this subject is coming back again now that you are a grown woman!" - My Mom confusedly said.

"Mom, I understand how difficult, and crazy this may sound, but it is the truth, my truth, who I really am, and I don't want to hide myself anymore. I am tired of feeling afraid to accept who I really am, and use the abilities that I naturally possess, and which you also do, and you refuse to accept them because of fear! You are like me, and one of my missions is to help you bring awareness of your own true divine identity. There are many like us that volunteered to incarnate into this world to raise awareness, and help this planet move on to the next dimension." - I said.

"But I don't understand! I cannot picture how it's possible that I had you in my belly, felt you moving inside of me, and then gave birth to you! and you are telling me that you are like a little grey alien that came to this planet?" - My Mom said.

"I know that the whole world has this misconception that every being out of this world is a grey alien with big head, and big eyes. Humanity has yet to comprehend of what else is out there in this immense universe. We all have become so ignorant believing that we are all the intelligence that is out there.

There are many supreme intelligent beings with three dimensional bodies like us, and others that are made of pure crystalline energy easily undetectable by modern science. Unfortunately, humanity does not possess an open conscious awareness that is needed to be able to match their energy vibration, and be able to see them.

This is how I was able to incarnate into this world through you, as a crystalline pure energy being from a higher dimension of evolution. So yes! You gave birth to me, and I was in your belly, but everything was planned for me to be able to come to this world. I had to leave my high divine estate of consciousness, and my immortality to be able to incarnate into this three dimensional world at the risk of forgetting who I truly am, and my divine mission.

This planet will soon go through a major vibration/energy change in which many may not survive. This was the only way for us to do our work to save as many, and activate our brothers and sisters of light before the big change. It is time for humanity to raise their estate of consciousness to a higher level, and find balance within in order to have a peaceful future, or soon all the living beings of this planet will cease to exist!" - I said.

My Mom was so perplexed by all I said that she kept staring at me even after I stopped talking. She looked as if she was analyzing, and trying to bring some sense, and understanding to all these, and continued giving me a blank stare until she finally came back to reality.

"Well, I must say even though all you said sounds crazy, I confess that at the same time it makes sense. It really made me think about all the things that I quietly questioned myself when I was a child. I always felt that I never belonged here, and to my own parents. I felt so different, and often questioned God if he made a mistake in bringing me into this world. Of course when I found the proper moment, and time to ask my own mother if the reason why she mistreated me was because I was not her child, she would answer me back by slapping me on the face, and then punishing me. Maybe the reason why I had to come to this world was because it was the only way for you to come, and help me understand, and remember. It will take me some time to really sink all this within me. I now know why you always, since your childhood, questioned so many things about this world, and badly wanted to seek for your answers." - Mom said.

"I am glad that some of this is making sense, and I am not expecting you to absorb all this information right the way. I know it will take time, and work to raise your real awareness of who you truly are, but first you need to work on healing that wound from that emotional abuse from your childhood, and I and the divine angels will be there to help you always." - I said.

My Mom then broke into tears, and we hugged. I now felt that part of my mission had begun. It is now time for Daniel, and I to return back to the U.S., and it was another emotional moment. Part of my heart felt like it was being ripped from my chest cavity as if a part of my old self was left behind, and giving birth to the new being that I now am. I was crying so much in the plane looking through the window as we were flying away from my beautiful homeland.

We are now back in the U.S., and it took me about a month to bring myself back from feeling sad after we left my beloved country. My sense of awareness has now become more opened, and I felt that there was more to be done. For some reason, I kept feeling that I was going to disappear for a while, that something major was going to take place in my present time, and it was coming very soon. I began having very vivid dreams about my star family making their presence known on Earth, and that they were coming to get me. I continued with this vivid dream almost everyday for several months. I told Daniel about it, and he didn't know what to think of it. I said to him that I have this deep feeling that the dream is real, and that if it were to happen, I knew that I would be coming back to let him know that I was ok. He seemed a little fearful, and concerned for my safety, but did not say much.

On April 2012, we had the opportunity to fulfill one of our mutual dreams, and it was to go to Hawaii. We had tried to book a trip to the beautiful island of Hawaii for the past 3 to 4 years, but something always happened either not enough money, or no rooms available, because they had to be booked almost a year in advance. For some strange reason, we were planning our next trip, and decided to take a chance, and call my timeshare to see if they had anything available. To my surprise, they had two rooms available at different locations. The representative told me that I was very lucky, because nobody can ever reserve this location in such a short notice. We then immediately booked it. It was like a sign that we were meant to go there for a specific purpose, and I sure was thrilled to find out what the catch was. Like I always say, it is all about divine timing!

Once we arrived in the paradise land, I instantly felt an energy change that spiked at high altitudes. I felt like I was in heaven! We both couldn't stop smiling, and smelling the subtle scent of plumerias. We started our journey in Oahu exploring the commercialized island full of natural beauty, and old volcanoes. The next day we flew to the most beautiful island of Kauai.

Kauai brought in me a different sense of awareness. It made me feel at peace, and more balance within. I felt like a free bird exploring all the beauty. We began our tour by taking a helicopter ride, then driving around the island, and chasing rainbows over the most beautiful waterfalls I've ever seen. Daniel, and I felt so relaxed, and even more close, and in tune with each other. We were so much more in love with each other.

Our resort was located on a cliff with the view of the ocean. I would often sit on the grass on the cliff, and meditate to absorb all that wonderful energy, and at night time Daniel, and I would go to stargaze. My dreams about my star family coming to get me were getting stronger, and stronger the more we were there.

One night I deeply felt guided to go outside to the cliff to stargaze. I tried to convince Daniel to go with me since we only had one more night to stay, but he was too tired, and fell asleep. I then went on to put my pajamas on, and went to bed. I kept tossing in the bed, and couldn't sleep. The urge of going to sit on the cliff became stronger, and decided to leave Daniel in bed, and walk to the cliff alone in the dark. I sat in the grass, and closed my eyes inhaling the pure air coming from the ocean side, and then laid flat on my back to stargaze thinking, and wishing to have a chance to see, and meet my star family.

Thirty minutes have passed, and I decided to sit down again closing my eyes one more time to meditate for a little bit. I felt something strange happening in my heart as if my heart was charging with electricity, but was somehow comforting. I closed my eyes again to surrender to that feeling, then a sense of being engulfed in a warm loving presence surrounded my entire being. I then knew that I wasn't alone, but for some reason I still couldn't see anything. I kept staring at the night sky, and the ocean loving every sensation coming from it.

I heard a very gentle loving voice calling my name, but in the form of telepathy. I looked around, but still didn't see anybody when suddenly, I saw beautiful lights coming from the sky. Gorgeous lights of violet, blue, gold, white were coming from this silent ship. I was so astonished that I even forgot to breath!

The ship didn't land, and stayed suspended in the air but no noise was coming from it. I didn't know what to do, and looked around to see if anybody was looking outside seeing what I was witnessing. As I am looking around, I heard my name being called again, and I turned in the direction where my name was being called. The silhouette of a tall being about 7 or 8 feet tall began to approach me. He was beautiful made of pure crystalline blue energy with some kind of violet light coming from the center of his forehead. His eyes were golden white. His beauty indescribable.

"We meet again dear sister of light. Don't worry about anybody seeing us. They are all sleeping, and we make ourselves invisible to them." - He telepathically says as he is hearing my thoughts.

"I am so happy to finally be able to see you." - I said with a big smile.

"We are so happy, and proud for all you have done so far to help yourself accept your true divine origins. We have been with you throughout your entire journey, and we know how lonely, and frustrated you were at times. It was all about your planned growth process, and you had to go through all these moments in order for you to be where you are now, and we are very happy to have you back with us again.

It is almost time sister of light, and we must take you with us to be able to complete your remembrance of your true origins, and what you planned to do before coming to this planet. Long ago you told us to meet you here at this moment, and this exact place, because it is the closest to our vibrations and safer for us to make contact with you. Please don't be frightened for we know you have many concerns about your love ones." - He telepathically said.

"Thank you for being here. I can feel that my mission is a lot bigger than what I've imagined, and I know the only way to seek for more understanding is to go with you, but I cannot help to worry, and feel sad for leaving my husband behind. He will be devastated!" - I tearfully said.

"We know how you feel dear sister, for you will be gone for sometime, but it is necessary for there is a great shift coming into this world, and we need to fulfill our mission. Your love ones will be fine, and in time they will understand. You will have a chance to let them know how you are for you will be able to travel in a much less denser form, and soon you'll meet again." - He said.

I then smiled back feeling happy, and sad at the same time. My human side couldn't help to feel torn apart for leaving Daniel behind. I knew that once he would wake up, he would not find me, and would go desperate not knowing what happened to me. I could feel his heart being ripped apart in fear, and desperation. I didn't know how long I would be gone, and when I could come to at least tell him that I am ok, and that we would soon meet again. All these thoughts kept flooding my mind as I was being transported into the starship, and I knew my brother of light could hear my thoughts. Once inside the starship, I looked behind my shoulder leaving everything behind, and a tear came down my face.

"Dear sister of light, everything is going to be ok. You must stay strong so that your love ones stay strong. Remember, your feelings, and thoughts can affect how they feel for you are all connected. We are all connected. We love you." - He telepathically said as he puts his hand over my shoulder.

As the day arises, Daniel wakes up to find out that I am not in bed. He began calling my name, but did not hear an answer. He notices that the patio door is not fully closed so he goes outside to look for me, but could not find any sign of my presence. He begins to panic, and horrible frightening thoughts flooded his mind. He continues to search the entire resort, and still no sign. He then calls my cell phone, but the phone rings back in the room. The rental car is still parked in the parking lot. He then walks to the reception area to seek for help.

"Aloha! How can I help you?" - The front desk clerk asked.

"Hi. My wife is missing. I have looked everywhere, but cannot find her. Have you seen her?" - He anxiously asked.

"No Sir. She has not stopped by here. Maybe she went for a drive alone, or is in the pool area." - She said.

"No ma'am, she is not in the premises, and our car is still here, her belongings are still in the room, including the cell phone. I need you to call the police. She is missing! I am afraid she is in danger!" - Daniel loudly said in desperation.

"Ok Sir. I will call the Police now." - The clerk said.

"911 what is your emergency?" - Emergency dispatcher said.

"Aloha. This is Maulana from the Fountains resort, and I would like to report a missing person." - The clerk said.

"How long has this person been missing?" - The dispatcher asked.

"I am not sure. We believe since last night. When her husband woke up he couldn't find her, and all her belongings are still here. I am going to have you speak directly with her husband as he will be able to give you more details." - The front desk clerk explained.

"Hi this is Daniel Arriechi. Would you please send somebody over soon?" - Daniel asked.

"Mr. Arriechi I know how concerned you are right now, but first I need to ask you some more questions. When was the last time you saw your wife, and did you guys have an argument?" - The dispatcher asked.

"The last time I saw her was when we went to bed to sleep. We did not have an argument. We were loving every moment we spent together here. Please lets not waste any more time, and send the police to look for her now!" - Daniel said as he starts to get frustrated.

As soon as the police arrived, they began asking more questions to Daniel, and eventually told him that it is still too soon to report it as a missing person, because they need at least 48 hours from the time the person was last seen. Daniel became enraged and even more desperate. Hours, and days flew by, and still no sign of my presence. Now the police had reported me as missing. Pictures were posted everywhere, and on TV stations. I became the news sensation of missing persons titled "The Hawaiian Vanishing."

Four months have passed, and Daniel continued to maintain hope in finding me. He, and Joshua came together many times to try to find clues of what happened to me. My parents were devastated, and traveled to the U.S to stay with Joshua to help in some way.

Each time Daniel return back to our home, he would find himself crying in agony missing me, desperately not knowing if someone had harmed, or murdered me. As he tries to go to sleep, he recalls the day when I told him about my recurrent dreams where my star family came to get me, and begins to wonder if that is what had happened. Then he shakes his head in disbelief and takes a sleeping aid to help him regain some rest. As he is asleep, I was able to gently enter into his dream in the ethereal form.

"My love. I know how desperate you have been all this time, and I am sorry for causing you this pain. It had to be done in order to finally fulfill my mission. I just wanted to let you know that I am fine, and safe and we'll soon meet again. I will in time give you a sign where we can meet. Pay close attention to the news on TV for the world will soon be aware of our presence, and arrival. I love you with all my heart." - I said.

"Please don't leave me!! I miss you so much!!" - Daniel desperately screams, and suddenly wakes up to find an empty room again. He begins to question if what he saw in his dream was real, or not.

The same night I traveled to my parent's room. I made contact with Mom through her dreams in the ethereal form.

"Mom, I know how devastated you, and everybody have been feeling. I understand the pain, and fear that you are experiencing. I wanted to let you know that I am ok, and safe.

I have reunited with my star family, and this was the only way for me to fulfill my mission. I had to go away to relearn my true origins, and regain my true physical form. We will soon be able to meet again, but for now this is the only way I can communicate with you, because you will not be able to recognize me in my current form. Please pay close attention to the news on TV for the world will soon be aware of our presence, and our arrival. It is then when we will be able to see each other again. I love you don't forget that!" - I said.

The next day Daniel drives back to Joshua's house to meet for lunch, and to continue the search for clues. Daniel does not mention the dream, and message he received that night, and tries to ignore it. Suddenly, while they were eating, Mom brings the subject of the strange dream she had. As my Mom begins to describe her dream, my brother Joshua translates for Daniel. Daniel stops eating, and shows an astonished look on his face, and my parents couldn't help to notice him turning pale.

"Daniel! What's wrong? Are you feeling ok?" - Joshua very worried asked.

"Yes, I am ok. I am just shocked that your Mom, and I had the same exact dream in which Paula gave that detailed message. I remember several months ago, not too long before we went to Hawaii that she kept telling me that she had many recurring vivid dreams about her star family coming to get her. She said if that were to happen, she would somehow come to let me know that she was ok!" - Daniel says as he regains color on his face.

"Oh my God! She was here! She used to tell me that too. I can't believe it! She is alive, and well! - Mom shouts as tears of joy, and relief runs down her face.

My family held on to that message which gave them a huge sense of hope, counting the moment when we could reunite again. Meanwhile, my missing case was still open. The news continued to talk about the unsolved mystery of "The Hawaiian Vanishing."

On November 9th, the news began reporting massive UFO sightings all over the world. My family were glued to the TV waiting for signs from me.

People all over the world were frightened creating stories of a major alien invasion, or end of the world. The government, and military couldn't deny the obvious sightings, but continued to work secretly so that the citizens would not be aware of their plans, and possible attack.

NASA confirmed the military that they are also seeing these massive UFOs. They informed them that the flying objects looked like energy ships of different light frequencies. They also reported activity outside the sun with starships using the sun as a portal to connect to Earth.

The government, and military were now on high alert expecting the worse not knowing if they had the sufficient technology to protect the country, and the rest of the world in case of an attack. The citizens were now in fear, and desperate to get answers from the government. Now the President of the United States was forced to address the nation to bring some calm to the citizens.

"My fellow citizens. It has come to my attention all of your concerns with the current situation of the UFO sightings. We are aware of such sightings, and we have everything under control. Please do not panic, for these beings have not shown any signs of malevolence, and have not tried to make contact with us. We are doing everything we can to maintain the security of all of you, and of this nation. In the mean time, it is necessary that you all continue with your daily life responsibilities until further notice." - The President stated.

"Mr. President! Mr. President! is the military going to try to make contact with them?" - A reporter asked.

"The military is trying to do everything they can to maintain the safety of this nation, and at this moment no such plans of contacting these beings have been made. The matter has to be studied carefully before attempting to make such contact. Thank you for your attention. No more questions." The President concludes.

One month later, on the night of December 9th, while the President is alone rehearsing his next speech in the oval office, the room begins to shake. The President panics for a moment, but noticed that the secret service did not come to check on him and he continues on with his task. Suddenly, a big bright light surrounds the room making him so startled that he trips over the chair, and almost falls down. Again, he is surprised that nobody has come to check on him, and begins to question his own sanity when unexpectedly, he hears a voice in the middle of the room.

"Hello Mr. President."

"Oh my God! How did you get in here? Who are you?" The President asked in fear as he is trying to carefully reach for the panic button.

"Your secret service will not be able to hear you. We had put the rest of your people in a stasis mode while we make contact with you. It is for our safety, and their safety for they are not ready for our formal introduction. That is why we are here to talk to you. We know that you are very scared, and what your thoughts are for we can hear what you are thinking right now. Please don't be frightened. We are not here to cause any harm to you, or anyone in this planet."

"Who are you? How many of you are here?" - The President fearfully asked.

"My name is Araceda, commander of the intergalactic starship of light from the star system your people call Sirius B. I speak for the rest of my family of light for you are unable to see them at the moment. Some of us do not possess denser body forms like you, for we all come from different intergalactic systems.

Together we all formed the Galactic Federation of light to maintain the peace, and unity of all intergalactic systems. We have been watching your world for millions of years, and for thousands of years we have come down to make contact with your ancient civilizations. Together with many of my brothers, and sisters of light have come down to incarnate within you as humans beings for the last hundreds of years. It was the only way for us to continue to do our work without being detected. This is why you can see me in the human form. Our bodies are made of pure crystalline blue energy from the tenth dimension."

"Jesus Christ! I can't believe this is happening! What do you want from us? Why are your ships here?" - The President asked with a very panicked look on his face.

"We want you to address your nation, and the entire world of our presence, and contact. We want you to prepare the world for our arrival. We come in peace, and all we want is for all your people to remember who we are, and how we are all connected. We don't mean to cause fear, and your job now is to make sure that your nation, and the world stay calm during our arrival. We would like you to prepare Cape Canaveral for our descend, and prepare everyone to be present. The date will be December 21st of your present year."

"But wait! how many of you......." - The President tries to ask soon realizing that now he is all by himself.

The secret service hears the President trying to ask something loudly, and opens the door.

"Mr. President is everything ok? - The secret agent asked.

"Yes, everything is ok. We have to address the nation. The alien visitors have finally made contact."

- The President said with a very alarmed look on his face.

PART 7 : *THE DISCLOSURE*

SEVEN

Several days have gone by since the night of the first contact, and the President is still in disbelief of what had happened the night December 9th. He still remains concerned of how he would address the nation, and the world about the extraterrestrial contact without causing significant panic or chaos to all the citizens, and worldwide nations. The Pentagon, and the Joint Chief of Staff have now been informed of the extraterrestrial contact. The security of the nation, and of the world have been raised to high alert. Leaders of all the nations in the world were soon going to be informed of the Contact during an emergency meeting at the U.N.

"Welcome Leaders. Thank you all for being here in such a short notice, but it was necessary for what I'm about to tell you is of major importance, and possible danger to our world....our planet. As you all are aware now of the worldwide UFO sightings that have been happening for the last several months, I am afraid to inform you that these visitors are not here to just observe us, but they are in fact planning to land in our home planet. They have made contact with us.." - The President of the U.S explained with a very worrisome tone on his voice.

The whole room goes silent for a few seconds with all the leaders of the nations looking astonished, and with disbelief of what they are hearing from the President of the United States. Suddenly everybody begins to talk at the same time, and the whole room gets loud. Some in panic, and some in disbelief.

"Mr. President, I am not sure how to take this information you are giving us..Is this a joke? What do you mean when you say "They made contact with you"? Please explain, because this sure does not make any sense!" - The President of Russia angrily asked.

"I know how crazy this may sound, and I have no way to prove that they made contact with us. Believe me! This is not a joke, nor some sort of game to cause chaos amongst nations! I would like for us all to work together in unity in case of an attack to our home planet. These beings have the ability, and technology to appear, and disappear without being detected by our current technology.
I was contacted on the night of December 9th in the oval office by this being whom she called herself Araceda. While my staffs of security were outside my door, she beamed herself down without being detected by my staff, or security cameras! She told me that they have the ability to put people in a "stasis mode" for their protection while they made

contact with me. Now you can imagine how vulnerable we all are against their technology! Although she reassured me that they are here in peace, and would like for us all to remain calm during their landing, we must be prepared for the worse. Soon, I will be addressing the nation of the contact, and you all should do the same too. We have to try our best to keep our people calm during this moment in history, and we must cooperate for what they ask. Their plan is to land on Cape Canaveral on December 21st of this year." - The President the U.S explained.

"So where are these beings from, and what do they want from us?" - The Prime Minister of the U.K with a very concerned tone on his voice asked.

"All I can say is that this being told me that they have been watching our world for millions of years, and have made previous contact with our ancient civilizations. For thousands of years, they have been incarnating within us as human beings to do their work in the planet without being detected. I must warn you, this being looked very human to me, but she informed me that she was incarnated as a human being. She explained that her real form is not dense, and three dimensional like our bodies, but instead made of crystalline energy from the tenth dimension from the star system of Sirius B. She added that there are many other beings with them from other intergalactic systems to which together they call themselves The Galactic Federation of light." - The President explained.

"So, what do you suggest we all should do?" - The Prime Minister of the U.K asked.

"I suggest you all to stay calm, and for us all to work together. Our priority is to maintain security of our world. My Joint Chief of Staff is currently working hard to prepare our military in case of an attack, and very soon you all will receive further notification from my staff of defense on how we can coordinate our move. I will soon be addressing the nation of this contact. The world has to be ready for their landing. Until further notice, please do not attempt to do anything against these beings. We must remain in peaceful negotiation, and do as they ask for the moment until we make sure of their true intentions." - The President of the U.S said.

On December 15th, the President of the United States does a live announcement on all TV stations addressing the nation, and the world of the contact, and plan of landing of the extraterrestrial beings.

"My fellow Americans, and citizens of all the world, I am here to inform you of an event never experienced in our modern history. As you all are aware of the current UFO sightings all over the world going on for several months now. It is my duty to inform you all that the extraterrestrial visitors have finally made contact with us. I was contacted by a being named Araceda, commander of the intergalactic starship of light from the star system of Sirius B. They have plans on landing on U.S grounds on December 21, 2012. I know how you all might be frightened right now, but I can reassure you that we, and all the leaders of the world are working together diligently to maintain the safety of our planet, and of our people. It is my advice that you all stay calm, and do not attempt anything that might endanger the safety of our world.

I have now declared Martial Law. Anyone that might attempt using unauthorized weapons against these beings will be punished adversely by law enforcers. These beings have reassured me that they are here in peace, and with no intentions of causing harm to us. I am expecting all of you to do the same for them unless instructed otherwise by us." - The President explained.

The whole crowd of reporters in the room are now desperately asking questions at the same time, and wanting to have the first live Q & A for their TV news stations. All of their faces filled with fear, but at the same time focus on their task of getting their questions answered for ratings.

"Mr. President!! Mr. President!! Please tell us how....." Several news reporters asked at the same time.

"Please try to calm down I can only answer one question at the time." The President demanded.

"Mr. President, where in the U.S are these beings planning to land, and what is their purpose for landing?" - A CNN reporter asked.

"The being that call herself Araceda, informed me that they are planning to descend on Cape Canaveral on December 21, 2012. I am not certain of the actual intentions for their landing. All I could understand is that they want us all to remember who they are, and how we are all connected. They want our world to know their existence. So far she did not seem malevolent. Next question, please." - The President said.

" Mr. President you refer to this being "Araceda" as a she. How do you know she is female? What does she look like? - Another reporter asked.

"Well, because this being looked 100% human to me....." The President tried to explain when he gets interrupted by the massive commotion of voices from the shocked crowd.

"Please everybody remain calm, or we will be forced to end the session soon" - The Senior Advisor of the President interceded.

"As I was trying to explain, Araceda looked very human to me. She explained to me that the reason why I was able to see her in that form was because she was incarnated on Earth as a human being to do her work on our planet. In fact, for thousands of years many of them have been incarnating amongst us as human beings to avoid detection. Their body is composed of crystalline blue energy, and it is not dense like our bodies. This is how they can beam themselves anywhere they want. Next question." - The President added.

"Mr. President, so you are telling us that these beings have been living amongst us all this time, and we did not know about it? What kind of work exactly have they been doing here on our planet? Does this have anything to do with the so called Roswell incident, and area 51? - A reporter asked.

"Yes, unfortunately these beings have been living amongst our civilization without our knowledge. As of now, we are not exactly sure what kind of work they have been doing to our planet all this time, and what exactly they are trying to hide from us. My staff of defense, and I are working diligently to find answers, and maintain security of our world. I wish I would have more details on this matter, but this is how much this being was able to tell me. Please stay tuned until further notice. No more questions." - The President concludes.

"Wait! Mr. President! Mr. President!! - A few more reporters tried to ask as the President leaves the podium.

"The President has now concluded his Q & A session. Please no more questions until further notice." - The senior advisor of the President exclaimed.

Everybody in the whole world were now in shocked, and fear after the President of the United

States gave his worldwide announcement. People began preparing themselves by building underground shelters, and stocking food supplies for the possibility of an attack. Some people began making posters, and walking on the streets to announce the "end of days" as predicted by the Mayans. Others were holding banners, and parking their RVs in parks, the Mayan ruins, and other open places to welcome the extraterrestrial beings. The world's reaction was now being televised by news stations all over the world with the countdown for the E.T's arrival. Daniel, Joshua, Mom, and Dad, were now aware of the disclosure of the extraterrestrial contact, and now they knew that this was the sign that they were anxiously waiting for.

"Daniel we must go to Cape Canaveral! This is the sign that Paula was telling us about!" - Joshua insisted.

"I think you are right Joshua. We must go there, but the only problem is how close we can get, and if we can even get inside. I am very sure the whole area is going to be heavily guarded by the military." - Daniel said.

"Where is Cape Canaveral? - Mom asked Joshua.

"It is East of Florida probably about 18 to 22 hours driving from Ohio." - Joshua said.

"Well, wouldn't it be easier to fly there instead of driving?" - Mom asked as Joshua is translating for Daniel.

" I am not sure if the government is allowing any commercial planes to land in Florida, or near the area at this moment, but I'll sure check. If in the event that there are no commercial flights to Florida, we can always fly to Atlanta, and rent a car to drive down to Cape Canaveral. I believe it takes approximately 8 hours driving from Atlanta." - Daniel said.

"That sounds like a great idea!" - Joshua said.

PART 8 : THE ARRIVAL

EIGHT

The world is now on high tension, and as the days go by, there is a sense of energy change in the air. People began to act irrationally led by their fear of what could happen once the extraterrestrial beings touch land on the planet. There is so much chaos amongst people, so much anger, and violence. No one, not even the government could guarantee the safety of the planet, and it's people.

The mortality rate around the globe has been increasing significantly since the day of the disclosure, and a high percentage of it due to suicides from people that were severely overcome by their own fear of the unknown. Not only the government had to deal with the possibility of an alien attack, but also unusual changes within the planet itself. Scientists have now discovered that the Earth magnetic field is changing at a very alarming rate. They are puzzled as to what could be causing it, and at the same time they are beginning to question if the alien visitors are the ones to blame.

"Sir! The magnetic field of the planet is changing drastically since the alien visitors made contact with us. We are not sure what could be causing it, but we are certainly afraid that if it continues to go the way it's going, it will definitely cause major problems within the core of the planet, and consequently create instability within the tectonic plates, more volcanic eruptions, and the possibility of atmospheric disturbances. We could lose all our satellite communications!" - One of the geophysicist informs the Chief of Staff of the President by phone.

"Are you aware that what you are telling me could lead to catastrophe? How sure are you of these findings? Is this reason why we are seeing so many light phenomena in the sky, or as you scientists call it ' Aurora Borealis'?" - The Chief of Staff of the President responded.

"Sir, my colleagues, and I are 100% sure that the magnetic changes are real, and getting worse as we speak, and yes! the Aurora Borealis is the first sign for this change as the poles begin to shift. This is just the beginning, and it could mean disaster to our world." - The geophysicist affirmed.

"My Lord! I can't believe this is happening. Thank you for your information. I will urgently communicate this to the President." - The Chief Staff of the President exclaimed.

While the President of the United States is in a meeting with the Joint Chief of Staff, and other military personnel from the Pentagon, his Chief of Staff enters the room, and whispers to the President. At first, the President didn't show any sign of interest for what his Chief of Staff was trying to inform him until he insisted of the urgency of the subject. The President now gets up, and excuses himself from the meeting for a moment and walks to a more private area to listen more carefully to what his Chief of Staff had to tell him.

"Sir, I apologize for interrupting your meeting for I know there is a major threat to the world." - The Chief of Staff exclaimed.

"Please get to the point." - The President in a state of tension, and stress said.

"Mr. President, we received a phone call from one of our geophysicists informing us of major disturbances in the magnetic field of the planet. They don't know what is causing it, but they have noticed that the changes have been spiking ever since the alien visitors have been showing up in our planet."

"So what does that mean for our planet? What kind of effects are we to expect to happen as of now? - The President asked with a very puzzled look on his face.

"Sir, it will mean total catastrophe to our planet as we know it. It means that there is a high chance that the poles will shift, and as a consequence, we will experience severe seismic activity as the tectonic plates begin to move, and the possibility of atmospheric disturbances." - The Chief of Staff of the president exclaimed.

"Oh my Lord! The threat to our world is worst than what we anticipated!" - The President now in a state of panic exclaimed.

The President now heads back into the meeting, and stands at the end of the oval table where everyone was sitting. His face looking pale as he is trying to digest all the information that was given to him. Everybody now is looking at him not knowing what was wrong with the President.

"Sir, are you ok? - The chief executive officer asked.

"Ladies and Gentleman, I was just now informed of another threat to our world. Things are worse than what we thought, and we have now reached a very critical point to the safety of our world. My Chief of Staff informed me that our scientists have discovered severe changes on the magnetic field of our planet. They are not exactly sure what is causing it, but they have noticed that the changes have been spiking ever since the extraterrestrial visitors made contact with us. What this mean to our world is that if the magnetic field continues to be unstable, it will eventually cause the poles to shift, and lead to total catastrophe." - The President stressfully exclaimed.

"So are you telling us that these aliens are causing this? - The chief executive officer asked.

"No. I'm not saying that, but it could be a possibility. There is too much coincidence for what is currently happening, but otherwise, we should prepare for the worse. We really don't know what they are capable of doing, and for that reason we must comply for what they ask until we make sure of what their intensions are." - The President affirmed.

"Do you have any idea of how the world will react once they know this information? We will lose complete control of the people!" - Another staff of defense exclaimed in anger, and in panic.

"The world doesn't need to know this information for it will cause more chaos, and potentially react in anger against the visitors. This information is strictly confidential, and should not leave this room. We are now, more than ever on high alert, and we must act cautiously when dealing with these beings. Any wrong move could lead us to global annihilation." - The chief executive officer exclaimed with authority.

Changes in the planet begin to take more effect as the days go by, and people are unaware of what the government now knows. The whole world begins to experience more seismic activity, more floods, more weather changes, and more death. People are now also experiencing changes within themselves as cosmic radiation penetrates more the atmosphere. Some are beginning to experience disorientation, nausea, head pressure, seeing, and hearing paranormal phenomena. Others are experiencing changes in behavior feeling of aggression, sorrow, and feeling of abandonment. Everybody seems very confused for what is happening, and no one knows what to think of it.

News all over the world are constantly reporting more natural disasters, and they are beginning to question if the government is not fully disclosing what is currently happening. They now begin to search for answers, and try to find people within the government that can secretly release the information to them. After so many unsuccessful attempts, they create their own conspiracy theory. People are now more curious to hear about it, and everyone is glued to the TV news including Daniel, Joshua, Mom, and Dad.

"Thank you all for watching CNN news. I'm Walter Schultz, and we are now Live with more coverage with the current happenings around the world as we count down the arrival of the extraterrestrial visitors. Go ahead Lisa, what do you have for us?" - The news anchor said.

"Thank you Walter. We have been very unsuccessful in trying to have anybody from the government to release us any information regarding the global natural disasters that we have been experiencing. Other sources have been drawing their own conclusions as they believe the extraterrestrial visitors are the ones to blame for these massive seismic changes. Some are believing that the aliens have built underground weapons to destroy us. In the end, no one knows for a fact what is causing all these global changes. We can only anxiously wait for the extraterrestrial visitor's landing, and pray for the salvation of us all. This is Lisa Brown reporting Live from Washington."

Daniel, Joshua, Mom, and Dad are now even more concerned if they will be able to find a way to enter Cape Canaveral. After listening to the news, they begin to believe that the government is hiding something of major impact to the world. Now more than ever, they begin to prepare their belongings, and head to East Florida. Mom is now in more fear than she's ever been.

"What if something happens to us while we are on our way to Florida? I am so afraid that there will be a massive earthquake, and kills us all, or worse the government shoots us for trespassing the area!!!" - Mom exclaimed in horror as she begins to cry.

"Sweetheart! Everything will be ok. Don't you let your guard down now! Think of Paula, and that we will soon see her again. Paula wouldn't have told us to meet her there if she knew there was danger. I know she will protect us." - Dad said as he tries to comfort Mom.

"Dad is right Mom. I know Paula knew ahead of time that it was going to be safe for us to be there. She will not let anything happen to us, but now we must remain strong! We are getting closer, and closer for their arrival, and soon we will reunite with her." - Joshua affirmed.

Meanwhile Daniel is just staring in complete confusion as to what is happening with the three of them. He tries his best to understand from the little Spanish that he knows, and gets even more confused as Joshua forgets to translate for him.

"Joshua! What is going on? Is everything ok? Why is your Mom crying?" - Daniel asked very concerned.

"Sorry, Daniel. I keep forgetting you don't understand Spanish. Mom was crying because she was panicking for us going down to Cape Canaveral. She is scared that something will happen to all of us on our way there. But she is ok now. We must hurry up, and get started. Did you get the tickets? - Joshua said.

"I understand how she feels for there is a lot of reasons to worry about, but I have faith that we will be ok. The tickets are ready, and we must leave soon. Our plane leaves in about 6 hours, and we will have a car ready for us in Atlanta." - Daniel said.

"Excellent!" - Joshua said.

It is now December 20, and the military begins preparing the area for the visitor's arrival. Everyone is on high tension, and fear as in approximately 24 hours, the world will soon know what the visitors intentions are. The whole world is expecting the worse. People from all areas of the country, and of other countries begin building tents close to the area of landing. There was so much commotion that the military became concerned that the civilians could jeopardize their plan of peaceful negotiation with the visitors. News reporters from all over the world were now flooding the area interviewing the civilians in tents, and trying to get a word from the military.

As the hours pass, the President is now more anxious, and scared of what exactly would happen once the visitors make landing. He begins to doubt the words of peaceful contact that Araceda promised to him. His fear overcomes his sense of trust, and makes a call to his staff of defense.

"Officer, how are we doing over there? Is everything under control? How many military staff are covering the area now?" - The President asked as he tries to get some security from all this.

"Sir, everything seems to be going as planned. We have 360 degree coverage of the entire area, and beyond. So far we have several thousand military soldiers of the best caliber guarding the area, and in a few hours we are expecting hundreds more to arrive. Our weapons are clear, and ready. The only concern we have is that there are many civilians surrounding the area in tents, and RVs." - The chief executive officer confirmed.

"How many civilians are we talking about?" - The President asked with a little concern.

"Sir, we believe there are approximately 10,000 civilians, and more are arriving as we speak." - The chief executive officer said.

"That is something of major concern officer. We need to make sure that they don't trespass the landing zone for it could be disastrous. How are all behaving as of now?" - The President said.

"The civilians are very calm right now, but we expect things will change on the arrival day. We are currently placing fences all over the area, and military staff to guard every entrance to prevent the civilians from entering the landing zone." - The chief officer said.

"Excellent. Keep up the good work, and I pray that we will not need to use any weapons against these beings." - The President said.

"Thank you Sir. We are also praying for the same thing. May God help us all." - The chief officer said.

The day that everyone has anxiously been awaiting for has finally arrived. It is December 21, the day in which the beings from out of this world announced that they will be landing on U.S land. The world awaits in suspense for the arrival of these beings. News reporters have Live coverage of the landing site. The whole crowd of civilians camping near the area are in mass hysteria as the hours pass by, and no signs of the extraterrestrial beings. The military personnel are on high alert, and stress as the mass crowd of civilians begin to lose control. They try their best to calm down the crowd, but are unsuccessful. The President finally arrives in the landing site, and notices the civilians going out of control, and decides to talk to the crowd to see if it brings some calm.

"My fellow Americans, I am truly impressed by your courage, and I admire the fact that you all came to this area despite of what could really happen here. I am aware that we have civilians from all over the world here with us in this truly remarkable moment in history. I welcome you, and I thank you for your courage in joining us. I know how desperate you all are for answers as to when they will be here. To tell you the truth, I don't even know. None of us know what time they will arrive for the being that contacted me did not disclose a time. I guess these beings don't have the technology to create clocks." - The President said as he is tries to appease the crowd.

The crowd then laughs, and begins to cheer the President. Now everyone is calmed as they patiently wait for the beings to appear. It is almost 3:00 pm, and Daniel, Joshua, Mom, and Dad are about 30 minutes from the landing site. They begin to see massive amounts of vans heading to the area, and it is then when they realize that they will have a very slim chance to get as close as possible to the actual landing site. As they get closer and closer to the area, the ground suddenly begins to violently shake for a few seconds.

"Oh my God!! Oh my God!! Divine Virgin Mary please protect us!! – Mom yelled as she begins to panic, and cry.

"Holy crap! What the hell was that? - Daniel exclaimed as he swerves the car trying to regain control.

"Holy mother of God! I hope we can make it there! - Joshua shouted in fear.

"Is everyone ok?" - Daniel asked as he looks through the rear view mirror.

"Yes, we are ok. My Mom is a little bit stressed out by all these, but I think she will be ok. How much longer do we have until we get there? - Joshua said.

"We are actually here. We have arrived, the only exception is that we have a long walk ahead of us for there are thousands of people, and cars here. We need to hurry. I have a feeling that they will be arriving very soon." - Daniel said.

As Daniel, Joshua, Mom, and Dad try to walk as fast as they can, and push themselves through the mass crowd of people, the sky begins to change, and a small gust of wind comes out of nowhere. The people sit in suspense as they feel something is happening. Meanwhile the President, the military, and all the leaders of the world are on high alert as they begin to witness different colors of light coming from the sky. Balls of energy of different light frequencies begin to descend, and the mass crowd of people are in awe for what there are seeing. Everybody stays unusually calm as they observe the balls of light flying all over, and checking the crowd from above. Daniel, Joshua, Mom, and Dad take advantage of the moment to move through the crowds, and finally make it to the front gate where there is a guard protecting the area.

"Sir, I am not sure if you are going to believe what I'm about to tell you, but we need to go through the gate. We have to be present in the landing site. The being that you all are expecting to land is my wife, and their daughter. She wanted us to meet her here. Please let us in." - Daniel explained

"I am sorry Sir, but I can't let you go in. We are not allowed to let any civilians in the landing site." - The guard said with a very authoritative voice.

"Please! You don't understand! We are her family!" - Daniel exclaimed as he gets frustrated.

"Please Sir step away from the gate!" - The guard begins to raise his voice.

Daniel tries to persuade the guard to let them in, and the guard begins to get more authoritative and angry. While they both continue to argue, the crowd suddenly begins to shout "They are finally here!" At 3:33 pm, the silent ship begins its descend, and the crowd is again in awe and fear. The President, and the staff of defense are expecting the worse as they head closer to ship. Everyone suddenly goes quiet as they see the silhouette of three tall blue light beings beam out of the ship. As they get closer to the President, and the staff, one of the tall beings changes its shape into the human form. Everyone still looking in amazement to what there are witnessing.

"Hello Mr. President. Thank you for meeting us here." - I said.

"Hi Araceda. It's is a pleasure to see you again. Welcome!" - The President responded.

"We know how afraid you all are about us being here. We know that you have your soldiers guarding the entire area with weapons in case of an attack." - I said.

"Noo...You must be mistaken. We know that we can trust you." - The President tries to affirm with a very shaky tone on his voice.

"Mr. President, we can see through you, and read your thoughts. We have known everything you have been planning for a long time. Please, don't be afraid for we are not here to harm you. Now, we will like to speak to everyone here for we have something very important to share." - I said.

"Please go ahead. We have the podium ready for you." - The President said.

"Hello brothers, and sisters. My name is Araceda, commander of the intergalactic starship of light from the star system your people now call Sirius B. We and many other intergalactic brothers, and sisters of light from other worlds have created the Galactic Federation of light, and our sole purpose is to maintain unity, balance, and love between all the worlds our universe possess.

We have been protecting your world, and many others from beings that have tried to break the balance, and destroy newly developed worlds such as yours. We are the keepers of your planet for we have been watching, and protecting your world for millions of years, and seen how each living being grew up, and developed to where you are now.

For thousands of years, we interacted with your ancient civilizations teaching them part of our technology, and helping them understand how we are all connected as one in unity consciousness. As time passed, we began to slowly detach from you in order to let you be independent, and grow freely as one. Unfortunately, we were very saddened to see how each of you began to grow separate, and filled yourself with greed, control, and power hunger. You began to destroy your own mother Earth, disrespecting every living being on your planet including your own brothers, and sisters. The balance of your world is now breaking, and your planet is now trying to cleanse what no longer serves it to adjust into a new higher frequency of love, and unity consciousness.

For hundreds of years many of us volunteered to be incarnated as human beings in order to do our work on the planet, and assist other brothers, and sisters in your world prepare for the new era of planet Earth. This is why you can see me in the human form, and there are thousands of us like me all over the world. Your planet, and many others within your solar system are now aligning with the galactic center of your galaxy, and your world will shift into the 5th dimension giving rise to a new beginning where all balance have been restored. Your planet will continue to shake its core more, and more as it reaches complete alignment, and as a consequence many of you will perish. For thousands of years, we tried to warn you of the consequences of your actions, but all of you, especially your government, preferred to continue the path of destruction in order to obtain more power, and thus install more fear within each one of you. You erased us from your history so you could continue to teach fear, and control over all of your brothers, and sisters. We are now here to remind you of our existence, and how we all are connected as one with God the creator of all.

Time is up for many of you in this world, and we are now here to bring on board many of our brothers, and sisters of light that volunteered to incarnate as human beings on this planet. In addition, we have selected many of you to come with us on board while your planet re-calibrates its frequency into the fifth dimension, and help you remember your true divine origins. Those who have telepathically heard our call will see one of our members of light, wherever you are, and be transported into many of our starships that are currently in position all over the world. We understand how saddened many of you will be for departing without many of your love ones, but we want you to know that you all are free to choose to come with us or stay, for we respect your own decisions. Those who will stay, will be reborn into a new era until you reach your own balance, and eventually reunite with your love ones for there is no barrier or time in higher dimensions.

My brothers, and sisters of light, it is now time for us all to reunite, and return home for our work here is finally done. We are very proud for all the work, and sacrifice you all made to recover your true identity, and help raise the vibrations of the planet in order to save many of our brothers, and sisters on this beautiful planet." - I said.

Once the speech concluded, all the people present in the landing site were in silence. There was an immense sense of fear, and guilt for what was happening. Some people were crying, and others in disbelief for what they were hearing. The President was in shock not knowing what to say or do, for he knew he was one of the people that was not selected.

"Please help us all! Now that we know the truth, we can change for the good! Please give us another chance, and help us stop the catastrophe that is soon to come! There must be something else you all can do to help us! - The President in a state of fear, and desperation said.

"Dear one, there is nothing we can do to help stop the process for it is part of the evolution of every world. Unfortunately, you all accelerated the process, because of your self destructive behavior, and your mother planet could no longer tolerate so much imbalance. You are all connected to the planet, and to every single living being in it just like the vessels that feeds every organ, and cell in your body. If you hurt one living being, or organism in the planet, you create wounds within yourself, and thus imbalance is created. Now you are all beginning to feel the pain you have caused to your own mother planet." - I said while placing my hand on his shoulder.

At a far distance, I began to hear a very familiar voice calling my incarnated name. "Paula!! Paula!!! - Daniel shouts. I began to smile as I was directing my attention to the gate that was heavily guarded by military staff. I telepathically ordered the guard to open the gate to let my Earth family in. As the gate opens, my Earth family runs towards where I was standing, and thousands of other people waiting on the other side followed in desperation.

"My precious baby!! I'm so happy to finally see you!! I missed you so much....I thought I will never be able to see you again, and have you in my arms! - Mom said as she is hugging me, and kissing my cheeks with tears of joy.

"Mom, I missed you all too. I am sorry for causing you pain, but it had to be done in order to fulfill our mission, and reunite with my star family." - I said as we were both embracing each other with so much love.

"My love! I felt so lost without you! I love you so much, and all this time felt like years for me." - Daniel said as he begins to cry out of joy.

"I am sorry for leaving you behind that night. Believe me, it was very hard for me for I knew how devastated you were going to be. It was all for a good cause. I love you with all my heart." - I said while we were hugging each other.

"So, What is going to happen now? Are we all going to die?"- Mom asked

"No, you are not staying here. You, Dad, Joshua, and Daniel are coming with me on board. The four of you are the reason for staying true to myself. You all gave me unconditional love, and support for everything, and accepted me for my true identity. Your hearts are so full of beauty, and so much love, and respect for everything. I am truly thankful, and blessed to have you as my family. Love, and respect for every living being is what is needed for the new era of planet Earth, and for that reason you are coming with me. Once you are on board, you will begin the process of cleansing to match the new frequencies of the planet, and then we will relocate all of you back into the planet." - I explained.

As my family reunites with me, one of my brothers of light places his hand over my shoulder, and telepathically tells me that it is time to go. I began to sense the fear, and desperation from all the people that were now present. I felt that soon they were going to lose control. We began telepathically calling all our brothers, and sisters that were selected. Many of them were in the crowd, and without hesitation, they came on board. The process towards the new Earth has now begun.

PART 9 : **THE NEW EARTH**

NINE

*T*he rest of the people were now crying, and shaking in sorrow, and desperation. They began to lose control begging to take them in. The military was trying to contain the people from creating more chaos. Me, and my brothers, and sisters of light, decided that there was one more thing to do before departing to lessen the pain, and fear from the brothers, and sisters that were staying behind. I shape shifted into my real form, and we began to form a chain of energy by holding hands in unity to create a energy wave of love, and calm to all the people.

The ground has now begun to shake violently as Earth, the Sun, and all the other planets in the solar system formed their complete alignment with the galactic center of the galaxy. The color of the sky begins to change as high cosmic energies shower the Earth. People begin to experience static electricity running through their bodies making them feel lighter, and less dense as if they were going to slowly disappear.

"Dear ones, please don't be frightened for what is currently happening now. This is not the end, your world is now giving rise to a new beginning. What you all are experiencing now within your own bodies, it's your body frequencies adjusting to the 4th dimensional frequencies. You will soon be able to see, and reunite with your long departed loved ones. Mr. President it has been a pleasure to have met you. It is time for us to depart now." - I said.

"The pleasure has all been mine, Araceda. Thank you for everything." - The President said as he is shaking my hand. Suddenly he turns his attention on a familiar silhouette coming towards him.

"Mom? Is that you?" - The President asked as tears run down his face.

"Yes son...it is me. I am so happy to finally be able to reunite with you again. Everyone here will now be able to reunite with their loved ones until we are ready to be reborn again. You see....this is not the end, my darling. It is the beginning of a new era for many others." - The President's mom said as she embraces her son.

"But you have been gone for so many years....how can this be possible?" - The President asked in disbelief.

"My darling, you are now sharing the same dimension where the spirit of all the departed ones are living. We were with all of you all this time, but you could not see us because your channel of understanding was not fully opened due to fear. There was never an end to anything not even after you died. Our bodies have been like a vessel that carry our souls in order for us to learn here on Earth. Once our destiny was partially fulfilled, we had to depart and leave our bodies behind in order for us to return again as human beings. The process would then continue until we are fully purified in our hearts, and spirits. It is then when we can move to a higher dimension where love only exists." - The President's mom explained.

"I can't believe this is happening. It is amazing!" - The President exclaimed as he is looking around him witnessing everyone reuniting with their love ones.

As I began to board my starship, I turned to look behind me one more time to the old place that once gave rise to the human being that I once was. I was thankful to have had the opportunity to live as a human being on this beautiful planet, but it was time to give rise to a new Earth full of so much more beauty and love never experienced before by any of my fellow earthly brothers and sisters.

Our ships are now going at full speed heading towards the Sun's portal that will lead us through the galactic center, and to the other side of the galaxy where a new parallel Earth is located. For many of the people on board, it will feel like many years have passed, but for us a split second. In our reality, time does not exist for it is just a limitation created by the human mind. In the new Earth, time will only be a memory of the past and soon will cease to exist.

"Dear ones, we are heading closer to your new home and soon we will begin our descend. Your bodies, and spirits are now cleansed from any impurities from the old world. You will now notice that your bodies are not as dense as they used to be for you will be able to teleport to different places at once. The fifth dimension has no limits like your old third dimensional world used to have. You will be more connected to mother Earth, and all other living beings like never before." - I said.

Once we landed on Earthly grounds, people began exiting the starships from different places. Everyone was running in excitement all over the place. There was a sense of so much love, and harmony. The sky was filled with so much purity and beauty with many colors of blue, pink, and violet. There was so much green, and beautiful flowers all over the meadows. All living beings, including animal life, coexisting in unity as one. It was a beautiful sight to see. I see my family so happy running with the other people which brought a big smile to my face.

Together with my brothers, and sisters of light, we began to slowly walk away from everyone including my Earthly family. It was time for us to board our starships, and return to our home star system. Suddenly, I heard my name being called from a distance.

"Paula!! Paula!!! Where are you going? Aren't you going to stay with us?" - Daniel asked as he is running towards me.

"No, my love. I have fulfilled my mission, and it is time for me to return back to my home star system. I will always be with you in your heart. Tell my family that I love them." - I said as I am placing my hand and caressing his face.

We began our departure, and as we are moving up in the sky I look out a window from above and see Daniel standing and staring as we were leaving. I could see my family running towards him and telepathically heard him explaining my parents of my absence. Then, they began to hug each other and wave.

Some time has passed, and I am now in my home star system ready to watch and protect other worlds as they began their evolutionary process. From moment to moment, I would think of my Earthly family knowing that somewhere deep within me I was missing them.

"Dear sister of light, we have noticed that your heart is not as bright as it used to be. We know that a part of you is still strongly bonded to your Earthly family." - One of my brothers of light said.

"Yes, my brother of light. I sense that a part of me is still with them. I feel that I must return for my feelings, and state of being are now compromised." - I said.

"We understand and support you, sister of light. We know that now it will be easy to contact each other when you are ready for us to come for you again." - Some of my brothers of light telepathically said as they all placed their hands over my shoulders as a sign of support.

I was now heading back to the New Earth and my heart was getting brighter and brighter as I was getting closer to my Earthly family. Once on land, I began to feel a sense of so much completion now that I was going to reunite with my family, and the love of my life. As I was watching my star family leave me behind, I began to think of the so many wonderful, and hard times that I had to go through in order to fulfill my soul mission. Some to which cause me so much pain, and grievance as a human being. So many times when I thought that I was abandoned by God, and that the world was crushing me. Times where my life was filled with hope once I began accepting my true self, and where love reined my life once again. Tears began running down my face, but this time, not for sadness, but for JOY. All the things that I once went through were not for bad luck but were meant to happen for a divine cause to make me stronger, happier, and more connected to God, and divine self. You see, everything has a divine plan, and for as much as we struggle to see underneath the surface, when the moment is right, and you are ready to embrace your true divine identity, and soul mission all the doors that once were closed, are now open.

The End.

CPSIA information can be obtained at www.ICGtesting.com
Printed in the USA
LVOW08s1731260514

387300LV00002B/522/P